Creation EX NIHILO

Thoughts on Science, Divine Providence, Free Will,
and Faith in the Perspective of My Own Experiences

Translated from Hebrew by
Jessica Setbon and Shira Leibowitz Schmidt

Benjamin Fain

Copyright © Benjamin Fain
Jerusalem 2007 / 5767

All rights reserved. No part of this publication may be translated, reproduced, stored in a retrieval system or transmitted, in any form or by any means, electronic, mechanical, photocopying, recording or otherwise, without express written permission from the publishers.

Typesetting: Pardes Publishing House
Cover design: S. Kim Glassman

ISBN 978-965-229-399-2

1 3 5 7 9 8 6 4 2

Gefen Publishing House
6 Hatzvi Street, Jerusalem 94386, Israel
972-2-538-0247
orders@gefenpublishing.com

Gefen Books
600 Broadway, Lynbrook, NY 11563, USA
1-516-593-1234
orders@gefenpublishing.com

www.israelbooks.com

Printed in Israel

Send for our free catalogue

CONTENTS

Preface — 7

Chapter One: Mind and Body — 13
1. The Inner Dilemma — 13
2. Freedom of Will—A Metaphysical Problem — 15
3. Materialism, Physicalism, Determinism, Reductionism — 18
4. Materialistic Solutions to the Mind-Body Problem — 21
5. The Three Worlds of Karl Popper — 26
6. Development of the World—Something from Nothing — 30
7. A Jewish Approach—The World Open to God — 33
8. Summary — 36

Chapter Two: Science — 40
1. Introduction — 40
2. The Principle of Induction — 42
3. Gödel's Theorem — 45
4. Immanuel Kant's Solution to the Problem of Induction — 47
5. Karl Popper's Solution to the Problem of Induction — 50
6. Man's Ability to Reveal Nature's Laws — 53
7. Scientific Cognition in the Real World—A Jewish View — 56
8. Solomon Maimon and His Philosophy — 63
9. First Conclusion: Science—Divine Revelation — 69
10. Second Conclusion: Science and Faith — 80

Chapter Three: Evolution of Life — 85
1. Introduction: Two Worldviews—Divine Providence, and a World without God — 85
2. The Basic Mechanism of Natural Selection — 88
3. The Molecular Basis of Life Processes — 90
   A. Proteins — 91
   B. DNA, the genetic code — 93
   C. RNA, the translation of the genetic code — 95
4. DNA>>> RNA>>> Proteins>>> Cells>>> Organism — 96
5. The Development of Life on Earth: Can We Prove the Theory of Evolution? — 100
6. Compatibility with Divine Providence — 103
7. Does a Law of Evolution Exist? — 105
8. Creative Emerging Evolution — 107
9. Conclusion: Evolution—Law of Nature or Divine Providence? — 112
10. A Conversation between an Atheist (A) and a Believer (B) — 115

Chapter Four: History — 119
1. Introduction — 119
2. There Is No Law-Based Regularity in History — 121
3. The Influence of the Level of Human Knowledge on Historical Developments — 123
4. Divine Injunction and Human Morality (?) — 128
5. Why Jews? — 132
6. Science and Jewish Civilization — 134
7. Evil Is the Antithesis of Judaism — 136
8. Human History—Providence and Freedom of Will — 140
9. Jewish Philosophers on "Everything is foreseen, yet freedom of choice is given" — 146
   A. Divine Providence and Freedom of Choice — 146
   B. Maimonides' Approach to the Problem of Freedom of Choice versus Divine Knowledge — 147
   C. Other Jewish Philosophers — 149
10. A Different Approach to the Paradox of "Everything is foreseen yet freedom of choice is given" — 155

A. Freedom of Choice—A Metaphysical Concept	155
B. Two Types of Development—Material and Spiritual	157
C. Knowledge of the Future	158
D. The Future Is Not Explicitly Concealed in the Past	161
E. Everything Is Foreseen	163
F. "I Will Be What I Will Be" (Exodus 3:14)	168
G. Summary	169
Chapter Five: Conclusion	**171**
1. Blind Faith versus Rationality	171
A. Mind and Body	171
B. Science	173
C. Evolution	174
D. History	175
2. The Self and the Quest for Meaning	176
Bibliography	179
Index	187

Preface

My first motivation in writing this book was to protect my own children and many other children, as well as youths and adults.

A child may acquire innocent faith, but when he gets older, he may one fine day meet an important person with an impressive appearance and a respectable academic title: PhD, or senior lecturer, or tenured professor. This person will claim that religious faith has been outdated for ages, and that modern science incontrovertibly *proves* the falsity of religion. The skeptical scholar will not explain or prove anything. He may use many vague terms, but with his impressive outward appearance, his suit and tie, and his academic degree, he may provoke questions of faith in our child's mind.

I fortunately find myself in a position to refute the doubting scientist. Although I may or may not be a better researcher than the doubter, I do possess many of the tools necessary to investigate this particular issue in depth. It is the confrontation of two worldviews that is the subject of this book: the secular view on the one hand, and the Jewish-religious view on the other.

Many people think that one who holds an academic degree, or a scientist with a reputation in a certain field, also has knowledge of the structure of science and of scientific discovery. Yet not every scientist who is expert in a certain field also understands the *science of science*, which includes the theory of scientific cognition. Albert Einstein, the greatest scientist of the past century, identified problems in the field of scientific cognition. Karl Popper, on the other hand, dedicated his entire oeuvre to researching the philosophy of science, and is considered the most important philosopher of the twentieth century in this field. In 1950, Popper gave a lecture at Princeton on the philosophy of quantum mechanics. Einstein went to hear him (as did Niels Bohr). As a result, Einstein and Popper held a number of meetings and lengthy discussions. I rely on some of Popper's research in this book. Understandably, Popper and others of his generation based their theories of the philosophy of science on the findings of their renowned predecessors in the field of general philosophy, such as Immanuel Kant and David Hume.

As a general rule, the scientist who claims to draw any kind of conclusions related to the nexus of religion and science must recognize the limits of science and its logical basis. He must base himself on the studies of the philosophers who came before him, from Hume in the eighteenth century to Popper in the twentieth. Only thus can he analyze the problem in a professional manner; otherwise he will err in amateurism, and despite all his degrees and titles, will prove nothing.

The purpose of chapter 2 of this book is to outline for the reader some of the basic tenets of science and to lay the foundations needed to analyze questions of Torah and science. Usually, people disregard the fundamental principles of science when they consider the seeming contradictions between it and Torah. This applies particularly to the contradiction between the physical history of the universe throughout its geological lifespan, and the biblical story of the six days of creation. Nathan Aviezer (*In the Beginning*) and Gerald L. Schroeder (*Genesis and the Big Bang*), among others, have written studies of this issue.

In my view, the literal meaning of the book of Genesis is not the only path to understanding the Torah and its relation to science, nor is it the most efficient. Rabbi Joseph B. Soloveitchik, a key Jewish philosopher of the twentieth century, chooses to ignore the difference between the scientific description of the evolution of the universe and the description of creation as it appears in the Torah: "I have never been seriously troubled by the problem of the Biblical doctrine of creation vis-à-vis the scientific story of evolution at both the cosmic and the organic levels, nor have I been perturbed by the confrontation of the mechanistic interpretation of the human mind with the Biblical spiritual concept of man" (*Lonely Man of Faith*, 7). Further, he writes about "Adam the first," at "the dawn of the sixth mysterious day of creation" (ibid., 19) who is aggressive, bold, and is perhaps a scientist or mathematician, and contrasts him with "Adam the second," who is contemplative, questioning, and irresistibly fascinated by his Maker.

The scientific description of the development of the world is on another plane from the biblical description of the creation of the world. The Torah's account has the connotation of a plan or an idea. "The world was created in ten utterances" (Ethics of the Fathers 1:5). Then each "utterance" is transformed into reality: "And God said, let there be light, and there was light" (Genesis 1:3). The Torah does not describe a process of implementation, but of planning, design: "let there be light," and then directly afterward, "and there was light."

Science, on the other hand, relates to the stage of implementation. Thus I see no contradiction between the plane of the Torah, which is the plane of divine thought and a divine plan, and the scientific plane of material, physical implementation. These two planes are unrelated. To use another kind of language, the connection between them is one of the world's mysteries. For this and other reasons, this book does not attempt to solve the contradiction between Torah and science (which I see as fictitious); many others have already written comprehensively on this issue.

As said, the focus of this book is an analysis of two worldviews: secular and Jewish-religious.

What do I mean by "secular"? One dictionary says: "not holy, unrelated to religion or to the sanctity of faith." The secular worldview is not uniform. In its extreme form, *materialism*, it recognizes only one aspect of the world: the material. All other facets, including our souls, are made of material. In its more moderate form, *dualism*, it recognizes the existence of two different entities: body and mind. (Popper's theory falls under this rubric). Neither of these theories recognizes the existence of a spirit that exists separately from the human being.

The first chapter of this book, *Mind and Body*, explains why materialism is irrational. The body of this chapter presents the Jewish view, which recognizes the reality of the spiritual *self* (as a person) that connects to the divine intelligence or infinite mind.

Chapter 2, *Science*, plays a central role in the book for two essential reasons. Firstly, science plays a vital role in human life, and so it is important for us to be aware of its limits. Secondly, none of the secular views propose a rational explanation for the existence of science or for our understanding of the world. This is in contrast to the Jewish approach, which offers a rational explanation for these phenomena.

Chapter 3 focuses on the *evolution* of life. The conclusion of the logical analysis I present there is that in contrast to the widely accepted view, there is no *law* of evolution. There are only phenomena of evolution, directed by divine providence.

In chapter 4, I present an understanding of the development of human *history*. Just as biological evolution is not governed by laws (chapter 3), no law or regularity governs human society over the ages. But human history is a different kind of development, directed by divine providence. The difficulty in understanding history is that of reconciling free will and divine providence. In the words of Rabbi Akiva, "Everything is foreseen, yet freedom of choice is given." Jewish philosophers throughout history have dedicated much thought to this paradox, and I will also attempt to contribute to its solution.

The scientist usually strives for objectivity. By "objectivity," he means that he tries to separate himself from the object of his research. He attempts to differentiate between subject and object. But this goal has a limit. In physics, quantum mechanics has set a limit to objectivity: the experimenter influences the research subject through the experiment itself. The very act of measurement has an influence on the object measured. True, objectivity is preserved so long as the scientist differentiates between his measuring instrument and himself.

As eminent twentieth-century scientist Erwin Schrödinger noted, the atheism of science is related in large part to its goal of objectivity. The scientist aspires to erect a barrier between his research and his *spirit* or his *self*. With his *intelligence*, the scientist endeavors to build a model of the objective, outside world. He cannot perform this monumental task unless he removes himself from his creation. Thus his creation cannot include its creator, nor does it have room for the Creator. This is the steep price of objectivity.

In this book, I have not attempted to remove myself in an artificial manner from the subject at hand. Divine providence and the Creator of the universe are the legitimate topics of the book, and the development of my own religious thinking is what led me to write it. I see no obligation to erect a barrier between my *self* and the discussion here. This means that I feel free to insert my *self* in the appropriate places.

Who can read this book? Anyone. Some chapters are easier to understand than others. The structure of the book is modular; the reader may study each chapter independently, without relation to the previous ones, although this leads to repetition in some places. Note that throughout the book I have separated detailed discussions of more difficult concepts into text boxes; these may be skipped over if desired. At the end of each chapter, the reader will find a summary with relatively simple explanations in popular language. In chapter 5 I give an overall summary of the book.

* * *

I am a scientist by profession, and this book is a scientist's view of reality, as free of preconceptions as I can make it. Commonly, scientists and philosophers, especially in the nineteenth and twentieth centuries, have held the preconception that they could explain the world in a rational manner without the divine. In this book, I will attempt to demonstrate the inadequacy of this approach.

* * *

I would like to express my thanks to the first readers of the manuscript of this book (Hebrew edition); to my wife, Shoshana, for her encouragement and criticism; to our son Gideon, for the initial editing and for many discussions on various topics that arose during his reading of the manuscript; to my daughter Eva and to Dr. Baruch Podolsky for Hebrew linguistic consultation.

Herzliya, Israel 5767 / 2007

Chapter One

Mind and Body

1. The Inner Dilemma

According to Karl Popper—one of the most important twentieth-century theorists in the field of the philosophy of science—the mind-body problem is the main focus of Western philosophy. (I will rely on Popper's philosophical analyses throughout this work.) Each of us humans lives and breathes this problem, whether consciously or unconsciously. Each one of us inhabits two worlds: an inner and an outer one. To put it differently, we all occupy two realms simultaneously, the private and the public. For now, we will set aside the question of the significance of these worlds or realms, and return to it later. Thus, we will attempt to grasp the meanings of these terms without entering the thicket of philosophical deliberations.

We are all directly and immediately aware of the inner self. I have a special relationship with my children, Aharon (Ron), Gideon, and Eva, and with my wife, Shoshana. I feel love for each of these people who are dear to me. I use the word "love" to describe my emotion toward all of them, even though my relationship with Aharon is not exactly the same as my relationship with Gideon, and my feelings toward Gideon are different from my feelings toward Eva. I am a believing man, so I try to love God "with all my heart, with all my soul and with all my might."[1] But rarely do I feel a truly intimate connection with God. On the other hand, never do I feel completely detached from God. I am commanded to serve God (this is both my inner feeling and my choice), which means prayer and study of Torah.[2] This commandment also includes the missions which define my life, including the writing of this book. I also worry greatly about the situation of the State and people of Israel. All this is just the tip of the iceberg of my inner self.

My inner world or realm relates to many individuals, living and departed; to memories; to pain, disappointment, failure, and sometimes, success. I assume that others also have their own inner worlds. But just as I cannot exactly describe my own feelings, such as the difference between my love for Aharon and my love for Gideon, I cannot arrive at an exact understanding of another's expression of his feelings. In the above, I have given a succinct description of my inner world. I am certain that this realm is real, that it truly exists and is not an illusion.

Another world exists that is quite familiar to us: the external world, the public domain. Everything in our environment is part of the external, physical world: tables, closets, computers, machines, cars, parts of my body (hands, feet, eyes, brain) and those of other people. They can be the subject of scientific study, and they can be the result of scientific research, as when technological advances lead to the development of new products. What characterizes objects in the external world is that there are multiple units of them, enabling us to study them. If something completely unique exists, it cannot be the subject of research. Research is not limited to only one place. Molecules can be studied anywhere on the planet as well as in space.

---

1 A believing Jew recites a declaration of faith twice daily. It is called the "Shema" and is followed by a paragraph that begins with the command from Deuteronomy 6:5, "*You shall love the Lord your God, with all your heart, with all your soul, and with all your might.*"
2 Torah is a general term including the Bible, Talmud, and many other traditional Jewish texts.

The external world belongs to the *public domain*. Anyone with the appropriate skills can conduct a study through examination and observation of objects in our external world. Here the special role of science comes into play. The accomplishments of science and its influence on our lives cannot be overstated. We often use the word "scientific" to convey the qualities of certainty, stability, and reliability. By contrast, the term "unscientific" is almost a pejorative.

Here we return to my (and your) inner world. This world exists only within my own private domain, and as such is not subject to scientific research. My inner world is "unscientific," meaning that the most important thing to me and to each one of us does not lend itself to scientific scrutiny.

A host of questions arise regarding the essence of the inner and outer worlds and the relationship between them. Many philosophers have invested great effort in attempting to prove that the inner world belongs to the external world, and that in truth, only one world exists, not two. In other words, my *self* does not exist. Only the material or physical world exists. While today, despite progress in science, we cannot read minds, the latter view maintains that one day scientific advances may enable us to do just that. In contrast, other thinkers believe in the existence of two separate entities having a reciprocal relationship. In the following chapters we will focus on the various solutions to the mind-body dilemma.

2. *Freedom of Will—A Metaphysical Problem*

Kiev, Ukraine, July 1941. I am eleven years old. The Germans have already invaded the (former) Soviet Union and are approaching Kiev. Many are asking themselves the purely existential question: What to do? Do we remain at home in Kiev, or do we evacuate and escape to the unknown? In actuality, only the Jews troubled themselves with such questions. My entire environment in Kiev was Jewish. I remember only one pupil who was not Jewish in my class at school.

All of our neighbors were Jewish, and the residents of Malaya Vasil'kovskaya, the street where we lived (the name has changed since then) were mostly Jewish.

For most of the Jews, the answer was clear: we could not remain in Kiev, as the Germans would probably arrive very shortly. But for others, the choice was not so clear. They were not so sure what would happen when the Germans would arrive. Foreboding rumors abounded. On the other hand, many remembered the German army in Kiev from the previous occupation less than twenty years earlier. The German soldiers were polite and civilized. In many instances, they protected the Jews from the locals. Many people had serious reservations about what would happen to them if they left. But my parents had no hesitation whatsoever: we evacuated in August 1941.

There was a pupil named Erlich in my class, with whom I had a special relationship. He was a quiet child, conscientious and talented. His family decided to remain in Kiev. After the war, I went to visit Kiev and learned that the Erlich family perished at Babi Yar, near Kiev. Some years ago, my son Gideon, my wife Shoshana, and I took a trip to Russia and the Ukraine, and while there we also visited Kiev and Babi Yar. There I told them about my classmate.

This is only one example of free choice—with life or death consequences.

Our entire life is a chain of choices, some more important and some less so. If my freedom of choice is taken away, I cease to be me. This is what I believe, and I am firmly convinced that this is so. However, philosophers who have devoted a great deal of time and thought to the issue of free choice have concluded that human freedom of choice cannot be proven, neither logically nor scientifically. It is a philosophical axiom that "a decision is made freely if the person is capable of deciding differently." This is problematic because we cannot reconstruct the exact conditions of a person's choice, in order to go back and see if that person would make a different decision. A person makes many mistakes and misses many opportunities over the course of a lifetime, and unfortunately, what's done is done.

The knowledge of free choice is not based on logical inference; rather, it is immediate, a non-mediated human experience. The philosopher Immanuel Kant writes this about free choice in his *Groundwork of the Metaphysics of Morals*: "To argue freedom [of will] away is as impossible for the most abstruse philosophy as it is for the most ordinary human reason" (123).

From the philosophical point of view, the concept of free choice is metaphysical. That is, it is impossible to prove the existence of free choice through experiment or by logic. Despite this, no rational human being doubts his ability to make decisions and to change his mind, to overcome his weaknesses and to act against his strongest instincts.

From a religious perspective, freedom of choice is a matter of faith. Freedom of choice is one of the most fundamental principles of Judaism. This principle is a necessary condition of the Jewish moral system. As Maimonides writes in the last chapter of *Eight Chapters—Introduction to Commentary on Ethics of the Fathers*:

> If man were not liable for his actions, the Torah's commandments would be void of significance and of its admonishments, and it would all be a complete lie, since man would have no choice regarding that which he would do. And thus all learning and scholarship would be nullified, as well as all works of art. It would all be vain and fruitless.... Though, the undeniable truth is that all of man's actions are devoted to himself. If he desires it, he will do it; and if he does not desire it, he will not do it...as it is said: "See that I have set before you today life and goodness.... I have set before you the blessing and the curse—and you shall choose life." (Deuteronomy 30:15, 19)

In the Babylonian Talmud, Rabbi Hanina expresses the principle of faith: "Everything is in Heaven's hands—except for the fear of Heaven" (Brakhot 33b). The interpretation of this is that man has the ability to freely choose to worship God or not. *Without the infrastructure of freedom of choice, Judaism becomes a collection of parables without normative validity.* "So what?" says the skeptic, who in any case does not believe in Judaism's principles. The answer lies in the fact that no moral system, including the secular moral system of Immanuel Kant, can exist without the principle of free choice.

We can summarize by saying that the principle of free choice is unscientific. We cannot prove its existence through scientific experiment or logic; rather, it is a metaphysical principle without which no moral system can exist. Freedom of will is *the* belief, without which the concepts of good and evil are void of meaning, and human life becomes pointless. The concept of morality is based on the concepts of good and evil, and thus would be irrelevant without freedom of choice.

3. *Materialism, Physicalism, Determinism, Reductionism*

The concept of materialism plays an important role in my life. Although I now live in Israel, I lived most of my life (forty-seven years) in the former Soviet Union. During those decades, citizens of the Soviet Union were required to adhere to a singular, uniform ideology—a materialistic ideology. From kindergarten through university and via the media we were educated in the canons and principles of materialism—*dialectical materialism* and *historical materialism*. We breathed materialism. A significant portion of our university studies was dedicated to the study of materialism. I took many courses dealing with Marxist materialistic philosophy.

On one hand, my chosen profession is the sciences: I am a physicist. The inner world, the spirit and soul are outside the bounds of a research physicist. In the field of exact sciences, materialism is one of the fundamental premises of research. Understandably, then, materialism seemed a perfectly natural option to someone like myself, and I would have to make a great effort in order to redefine my materialistic world view.

What is materialism? The metaphysical premise of materialism is that everything in the world has one uniform source which is material.

I phrase this carefully—I am not saying that matter is the source of everything. The word "matter" usually refers only to matter such as chemical elements, crystals, metals, or other substances, but not to such phenomena as light and sound. In other words, we can say that materialism refers to anything made from *materia,* where *materia* signifies any physical object. The primary claim of materialism is that *materia* is the source of everything in the world and is the one and only reality in the world. Everything in existence is *materia* or dependent on *materia* for its existence.

We could phrase materialist theory without using the Latin word *materia* and use instead the more modern and accurate term "laws of physics": *Materialism claims that everything acts in accordance with the laws of physics only.* Karl Popper calls the physical world "world one." According to the materialistic approach, world one is closed. It comprises its own reason for its development, independent of any external factor, and it is all-encompassing. This modern version of materialism is also known by the name *physicalism.*

Physicalism attempts to explain everything in the world, leading to the concept of *reductionism,* in which everything can be reduced to and derived from physics. Therefore, physics is considered the basis for chemistry. All the chemical elements and processes can be explained according to the principles, equations, formulas, and laws of physics. Despite the fact that chemistry deals with extremely complex forms such as the proteins of molecular biology, in principle we can describe chemical processes using physical formulas. Chemistry can be reduced to physics. The concept of reduction means that all chemical properties and processes can be derived from physical laws, though to be precise the possibility of reduction of chemistry to physics is only a belief—a belief based on many achievements of quantum chemistry.

The list below is a simplified representation of parts of the world:

(1) elementary and sub-elementary particles
(2) atoms
(3) molecules

(4) liquids and crystals
(5) plants, primitive organisms
(6) living organisms with senses
(7) self-conscious humans (that is, self-aware, conscious of self)
(8) society, state
(9) economy, free market
(10) science, art, religion, faith

The pretentious claim of materialism is reductionist, meaning that everything emanates from the properties and movement of *materia*. Everything in this world, every development in this world, including the development of life, is determined according to the laws of physics. In the list above, each row follows from the row above it; each row determines its successor. According to the reductionist claim, society and sociology can be analyzed and understood according to psychology; psychology can be analyzed in terms of physiology; physiology can be comprehended based on biology; biology is understood through chemistry; and chemistry is derived from physics. This means that, according to the reductionist approach, it is possible, in principle, to explain everything in terms of physics: life, human beings with feelings and desires, society, economics, and so forth. Euan Squires describes reductionism thus:

> This method [reductionism] always depends upon trying to explain the properties of an object in terms of the known properties of an object in terms of the known properties of its constituents, which are, in some sense, smaller and simpler. If this proves impossible then two reasons immediately suggest themselves: either the composite object contains additional constituents that we failed to include; or we did not correctly understand the properties of the constituents. [By implication there is no other possibility.] (*Conscious Mind in the Physical World*, 15)

This explanation seems convincing, but in actuality it says that reduction is *always* feasible. But we cannot prove this; it is a belief or metaphysical claim. Reductionism is, in fact, the primary message of materialism, or to be more precise, of physicalism.

Another important aspect of physicalism relates to the development of the world and of life over time. Basically, this aspect has two characteristics: deterministic, in which the past unequivocally determines the future; and non-deterministic, in which the past does not absolutely determine the future, but rather determines only the probability of various developments. These two possibilities are an inherent part of physics, and therefore also of physicalism. Therefore, if physics determines all developments, then they can be either deterministic in certain circumstances or non-deterministic in other circumstances. This aspect will be discussed below.

4. *Materialistic Solutions to the Mind-Body Problem*

I do not intend to review all the mind-body or body-soul theories, which are thoroughly presented by Y. Leibowitz in *Body and Mind: the Psychophysical Problem*, and in the monograph by Karl Popper and John C. Eccles, *The Self and Its Brain*.

In the materialistic school of thought, the mind has no independent standing. The laws of nature (and in the physicalism approach, the laws of physics) are the determinants of what happens in my soul. The mind is in the individual domain; I cannot speak in terms of "*our* mind." Physicalism takes a metaphysical approach to the psychophysical dilemma, in essence presenting the secular belief. Thus we cannot prove the validity or invalidity of this approach, but we can show that the materialistic approach does not agree with rationalism.

Haldane penned an argument against materialism in his book *The Inequality of Man*: "If materialism is true, it seems to me that we cannot know that it is true. If my opinions are the result of the chemical processes going on in my brain, then they are determined by the laws of chemistry, not by logic" (157). If our thoughts are the

> **Materialistic theories of mind and body**
>
> All materialistic (or "physicalistic") theories presume that the physical world is closed. The "parallelism" approach argues that chains of events occur in the brain, one event emanating from the other, in accordance with the laws of physics; and chains of events occur within the soul, also emanating one from the other in accordance with psychological rules. Parallelism defines a correlation between processes of the brain and those of the soul: each particular link of one event chain parallels a particular link in the other.
>
> The "identity" theory, one version of which is known as central state materialism, negates the existence of the psychophysical dilemma. This theory negates the concept of two interdependent entities. Instead, it asserts that the psychic reality is part of the physical reality. It could be said that the identity theory is the individual case of parallelism when the parallel processes of brain and mind are identical.
>
> In the distinctly materialistic theory known as epiphenomenalism, only the physical world exists. Events develop from each other in accordance with the laws of nature; and the psychic world—the mind or conscience—is a product of the physical world and a phenomenon occurring within it. Epiphenomenalism recognizes two essences: the physical and the psychic, with the physical producing the psyche. The psyche is only a phenomenon and has no influence on the physical, just as a movie has no effect on the movie projector.

result of a factor unrelated to wisdom or to our beliefs, then that factor is what determines our thoughts. In the materialistic approach, the movement of atoms and molecules in the brain determines our thoughts. If so, we cannot claim that the materialistic approach is rational.

However, the issue is not quite so simple. Haldane himself recanted his ideas in his article "I Repent an Error." The objection to his original explanation can be phrased as follows: computers act according to the laws of physics, and despite this they can act in full accordance with the laws of logic. The human mind can be represented by the brain, which we can compare to the computer. It is simultaneously a physical and logical being. Out of this comes the completely materialistic explanation of the mind, of the self. But Popper showed that this explanation is flawed, as he writes:

> I do not claim that I have refuted materialism. But I do think I have shown that materialism has no right to claim that it can be supported by rational argument—argument that is rational by logical principles. Materialism can be true, but it is incompatible with rationalism, with the acceptance of the standards of critical argument; for the standards appear from the materialist point of view as an illusion or at least as ideology. (*The Self and Its Brain*, 81)

Let us examine in more detail the idea of the human mind, the self, run by the sophisticated computer known as the brain. The mind's activities are logical events of the computer-brain. The mind has no separate existence; the computer-brain is all. Although Popper showed this materialistic approach to be irrational, it would still be worthwhile to devote more time and space to clarifying these ideas.

The idea that we are actually sophisticated computers is quite common. My university colleagues with whom I discuss such things are convinced that this is the case. Even among those who have not given any thought to the subject, most subconsciously accept the model of computer-brain = mind. The pioneering physicist-mathematician Roger Penrose made this very dilemma a central topic of his book *The Emperor's New Mind*. For decades, proponents of "strong AI" (artificial intelligence) tried to convince the public that in another century or two (some estimated as little as fifty years), electronic computers would be able to feel and understand the same way a human does. Penrose's book presents one of the strongest attacks on this idea.

The human self is variable and many-faceted: it includes feelings of responsibility, devotion, aesthetics, musical appreciation, jealousy, lust, love, fear, pain, creativity, and much, much more. Not everyone has the same powers of the mind. Some people lack musical ability, while others live their lives without ever experiencing love. But without a doubt, on the scale of emotions and experiences, religious emotions (love of God and connection to the Creator) occupy the highest order. I cannot accept the idea that all this could be contained in a box made of steel, copper, plastic, and wires; or alternatively, within a "mechanism made of protoplasm" known as the brain.

Not everyone is familiar with all of the above-mentioned functions. An atheist does not attach much importance to religious feelings. But no one would deny that everyone has a varying degree of musical ability, with very few instances of complete absence of musicality. On the other hand, great musical talents, such as that of a gifted composer, pianist, or singer are universally recognized. How is this connected to computers or artificial intelligence? We must conclude that the computer, as an alternative to the mind, must have great musical potential. Already, people have invented computers that compose music, though they do so according to programs devised by humans. Despite this, only humans can appreciate music. Music is pointless without a human mind to appreciate it.

In the list above of man's basic mental abilities, I didn't mention one important skill: the ability to think logically. Of all our capabilities, this one is most easily imitated by computers. Haldane's argument and retraction are related to a computer's logical activities. Is a computer truly capable of logical activity? Although a computer is initially programmed to execute logical actions, over time, mistakes are likely to confound the computer's action. This contradicts the argument that the machine acts according to the laws of physics and logic simultaneously. Sooner or later, all machines break down. In order to repair the machine, we must use logic. But the concept of logic is not part of a physical system such as the computer's hardware or the brain's protoplasm. Logic is a *concept of the mind*, as in the cases of music appreciation, love, jealousy, and hate. In other words, material properties and concepts are not enough to characterize the human mind.

We now return to the rebuttal of the original argument by Haldane himself: the computer (or the brain) simultaneously acts according to physical laws and the laws of logic. The response: the concept of logic does not belong to the material world. To examine, determine, or repair the logic of the computer's action, a human mind is required. Without the human's logical mind, the computer's logical function is completely undefined. The use of the term "logic" in the material approach toward a material machine is an improper application of the concept.

Feelings cannot be attributed to a computer, as previously stated. Thus the computer-mind model hardly agrees with the issue of free will. As stated above, free choice is a necessary element of the mind. Without free choice, no moral system, Jewish or otherwise, can exist. In the materialistic approach, chemical and physical processes in my brain determine my choices. My worldview and my feelings—logical or illogical as they may be—do not affect my choices. When physical processes are deterministic (the past completely and unequivocally determines the future), materialism totally negates free choice. In the case of non-deterministic processes, they are accidental. In this case, the quantum processes of the human brain have an important role, and the choice is also accidental. In both of these cases, free choice is negated. Thus, from this viewpoint, physical laws, not logical or moral standards, determine behavior.

In summary, the materialistic approach to the mind-body dilemma stems from the principle that the only world that exists is the world of *materia*. This world is closed, and all developments take place within it. No other world exists; a world of the spirit has no meaning in this approach. The world of the spirit is only part of the physical world. There essentially is no mind-body dilemma because the mind is merely an extension of the body, a collection of electrical impulses without deeper meaning or independent standing; it is only part of the physical world. This reflects the view of the scientist, whose research does not encompass the spiritual. Something that is known only to the individual cannot be a subject for scientific study, as science cannot investigate the private domain. This does not indicate a defect of science; rather, it means that science is inadequate in describing all of reality. Science's achievements are tremendous, but they do not have to blind us or negate the self within each of us.

5. *The Three Worlds of Karl Popper*

Now I return to physicalism and its relationship to the mind. Y. Leibowitz proposes that "a person attached to the physicalistic world view, which is based on natural science, and which attempts, justifiably or unjustifiably, to explain the world in its entirety, is not prepared to believe in the existence of something that digresses from the possibility of description according to the categories of physics" (*Body and Mind*, 44). On the other hand, when people observe themselves and their inner worlds, they have difficulty accepting the approach that the self has no independent status, and that the self is only a derivative of physical laws. This contradiction disappears if we recognize two worlds, an inner and an outer one, existing as two separate, independent entities. As Popper writes: "I am a realist. I claim, like any naive realist, that there is a physical world and there is a world of conscious states, and between them exists a reciprocity of influence."

I will present here an abstract of Karl Popper's concept of three worlds. World one is the physical world: the world of *materia*, in which the laws of physics rule. World two is my inner world, your inner world, their inner worlds. This is the world of self-awareness, the private realm; the world of subjective knowledge and our thoughts. Karl Popper claims that besides these two worlds exists another world, world three, the world of objective knowledge. This is the world of science, religion, philosophy, ideology, the arts, and so forth. Objectivity, for our purposes, refers to anything with independent existence—that is, independent of the thoughts of the individual. But this does not mean that objectivity is necessarily *truth*, nor can we always determine the truth.

World three is the objective world and influences world two. There is interaction and reciprocity between worlds two and three. In actuality, world two cannot exist without world three. For example, psychologists know of a few isolated cases in which a toddler has grown up without any contact with human civilization. In such cases, tragically, after a certain period of isolation, the child ceases behaving like a human being. World three influences world one, the physical world, in an indirect manner. Because of the reciprocal relationship between worlds one and two, we can conclude logically that world three influences world one. Physical theories (in the category of world three) may cause hydrogen bomb explosions in world one. The following diagram represents Popper's three worlds:

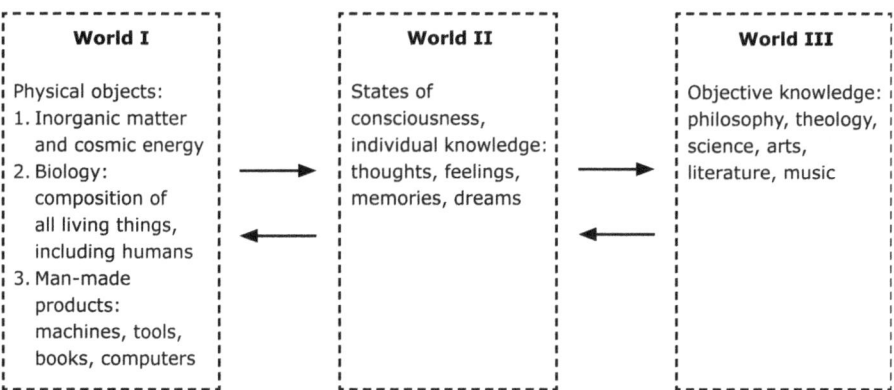

According to Popper, world three is man-made, although everything within it is autonomous. After a piece of music is created it has a "life" of its own, and has its own interpretation, independent of its creator. It is no longer dependent on its composer. In a certain way, Popper's theory is a synthesis of Descartes's dualistic approach (two distinct entities) and Plato's world of ideas. World three is similar to Plato's world of ideas in that it is not in space or time. We cannot define the space that Einstein's theory of relativity occupies or its duration. The difference between the two theories is that Plato's world of ideas has a divine source, while the source of Popper's world three is human, having a history and development.

We could simply ignore metaphysical considerations and presumptions and see the three worlds as a picture of reality. This would follow the *phenomenalistic* approach. This approach ignores the essence of things, and describes only the phenomenon.

Some emphasize the difficulty of the "three worlds" concept, particularly regarding the interactions between them. One response to this objection is that we also do not know what *materia* is, while we do know a great deal about its physical structure. Similarly, we do not know the essence of the self, even though we know much about the structure of the self. We know something about sleep and wakefulness, purposeful actions, problem-solving, virtue, heroism, self-sacrifice, devotion, selfishness, and so forth. All of these are phenomena, but do not explain the self in its entirety.

Many previously impenetrable barriers to human thought are now taken for granted since the twentieth-century revolution in theoretical physics by such seminal scientists and thinkers as Einstein, Bohr, Planck, Born, Schrödinger, Heisenberg, and Dirac. In the past, no explanation was acceptable if it did not contain enough tangibility and "concreteness." Such was the case with Newton's law of gravity, so aptly demonstrated by the so-called falling apple. Interestingly, today's science describes even the most usual substance only symbolically. We can roughly compare this to Jewish kabbalah or mysticism, which also uses symbolic language.

One of the difficulties of the dualist approach is the problem of interaction, the reciprocal acts of the mind and body. The body is material, while the mind is spiritual. How can they interact? To those versed in modern physics, this dilemma does not seem as difficult as it did in the past. In order to demonstrate this dilemma, I refer to a story told by Richard Feynman, one of the twentieth century's greatest physicists.

You can imagine to what lengths my father went in order to provide me a higher education. He sent me to study at MIT. I graduated from Princeton, returned home and my father says to me: "Now you have a good science education. I always aspired to understand something that I could never understand. My son, will you explain something to me?"

I answered, "Yes."

He said, "I understand they say that light is given off by atoms when the atom passes from one state to another, from an excited state to a state of lower energy."

I said, "That is correct."

My father continued, "And light is a kind of particle, I think they call it a photon?"

"Yes, that is correct."

"Accordingly, if the photon is given off from the atom, while the atom is in its excited state, then the photon has to be inside the atom."

I responded, "Well, that is not so."

My father said, "So how can it be that a photon particle is given off by the atom and is not there?"

I thought for a few minutes, then answered: "I'm sorry; I don't know. I can't explain it to you."

He was very disappointed. All these years he tried to teach me something, and the result was so inadequate. (*The Physics Teacher*, 1969, 319)

What's going on here? Here we have a clash of two ways of thinking. One is concrete, demanding concrete answers in terms of day-to-day experience. The modern physicist, however, understands that reality is complex and cannot be perceived in terms of day-to-day experience. The physicist is already accustomed to symbolic language. Feynman's father's question does not disturb Feynman. He knows that the spontaneous emission of a photon can be described by equations of quantum electrodynamics, and thus he has no need for a more concrete explanation. Moreover, the concrete explanation would not satisfy him at all.

This is simply an analogy. We have no theory of mind-body interaction, not in symbolic or any other language. We have no science that can describe the interaction between mind and body. But we have already stated that not everything belongs to the realm of science. The interaction between my inner world and my physical being is certainly out of the realm of science, as it exists outside the public domain and no science can reach the private domain. In any case, I have no doubt that interaction, or reciprocal activity, takes place between my mind and my body. I know it with certainty as an unmediated experience.

6. *Development of the World—Something from Nothing*

In contrast to the materialistic theory, Karl Popper emphasizes that the physical world, world one, is not closed. Rather, it is open to world two, the world of the self. From the secular point of view (to which Popper ascribes) no difficulty arises when we speak in the here and now. As opposed to the materialistic principle, which states that the physical world is closed, we can claim that the world in its entirety (worlds one + two + three) is closed, while the physical world (world one) is open. World one is directly open to world two and therefore indirectly open to world three. But philosophers cannot be satisfied with a momentary representation of the world. They must also consider the development of the world.

Secular belief as well as all scientific theories assume a stage in the development of the world when only the physical existed. *At that point, life did not exist, and according to secular belief, neither did the mind.* I emphasize this because it characterizes, and actually defines, the secular belief in contrast to the religious belief. Clearly the recognition of the existence of the mind outside of human life does not belong to the secular belief system. This is the antithesis of secularism; it is a religious belief.

According to the secular view of the initial stage of the world's development, before there was life, the entire world was world one, the physical world. According to Popper's scheme, world two is connected to life and to the human spiritual world, while world three is man-made. Now we must conclude that the world was open from the very beginning; otherwise it would be impossible to explain the development of worlds two and three. (Later in this book, we will discuss in more detail the creative development of the world, creating something from nothing). If the world was open in its primary stages, we cannot reasonably assume that it ceases to be open in the current stage of combined worlds one, two, and three.

What is openness of the world? By this, we mean that something can be derived from nothing (*creatio ex nihilo*). Things that did not previously exist can be created. This is the opposite of the reduction discussed in section 3 above. The well-known philosophical thesis seems obvious: nothing comes from nothing, *ex nihilo nihil fit*. However, the Jewish view does recognize the idea of something from nothing and relates it to the divine. As Maimonides writes in his *Guide of the Perplexed* (2:13):

> The first opinion, which is the opinion of all who believe in the Law of Moses our Master, is that the world as a whole, everything that exists other than God, was brought into existence by God after having been purely and *absolutely nonexistent*, and that God had existed alone, and nothing else—neither an angel nor a sphere nor what subsists within the sphere. Afterwards, through His will and His volition, He brought into existence *out of nothing* all the beings as they are, time itself being one of the created things. (Emphasis mine)

I suggest that a parable I have taken from physics is appropriate here. Invoking physics is legitimate and necessary in our time, since we have new tools available to us that were not available earlier. The Torah is timeless, but understanding the Torah and its commentaries is part of our general knowledge. Failure to use this knowledge, which also includes science, is unforgivable and unreasonable. The parable goes as follows:

> Basically, the entire physical world is comprised of matter and light. Now, let us imagine that we know nothing about the existence of light. Then we will "see" strange things take place in the world of matter: matter is not conserved, here and there matter is created out of nothing, and it sometimes disappears. The world is no longer strange when light is added to the picture. Light can create matter and matter can disappear when an atom goes to a higher energy state with the emission of a photon.

In this parable, matter represents our world and everything in it, including humanity and the human mind. Light is God.

According to the description of reductionism above (1.3), we can explain or predict the function of each organism based on knowledge of each of that body's parts. The ideology of reductionism, in essence, negates the claim that something new can appear with the development of the world. In contrast, philosophers such as Popper, who call themselves realists, cannot ignore the fact that in any secular picture of the world, new phenomena can be created during development. They do not retreat from the "something from nothing" idea. Later we will discuss new creation in the world. For now, we will say that worlds two and three were not part of the initial stages of the world's development (according to the secular view). They were created.

In the *phenomenological* description, if we ignore the essence of things, the "something from nothing" concept presents us with no dilemma. Although many philosophers hold a basic assumption that nothing comes from nothing, the logic of "something from nothing" is not defective. We have already seen (in Feynman's conversation with his father) that something can be completely unfathomable by common sense, but pose no problem for the scientist. When physicists understood that Einstein's equations or the Big Bang theory could describe something from nothing, i.e., the creation of the world, this was a great shock to many physicists. The equations describe only the model, a particular phenomenon of the world's creation which does not necessarily reflect reality. Scientists strive to describe reality, but are not always successful. In any case, in the model itself, the equations are not self-contradictory; they are logical.

Physicists have adjusted to the idea of something from nothing. Not long ago I participated in a seminar where physicists routinely used the term "something from nothing." It has become second nature, but this does not mean that the concept is now understood better than before. Suppose Feynman's father had asked him, "How can it be, something from nothing?" Then Feynman would have answered him, "I do not understand it."

But, again, this misunderstanding does not perturb the theoretical physicist; in his symbolic language of mathematical equations, there are no contradictions.

7. A Jewish Approach—The World Open to God

According to Judaism, "something from nothing," or the openness of the world, is openness to God. World one, the physical world, was open from the beginning and was created from nothing. "In the beginning God created the heaven and the earth. And the earth was without form and void; and darkness was on the surface of the deep. And the Divine Presence hovered upon the surface of the waters…" (Genesis 1:1–2). Moreover, according to the Jewish perspective, creation continually renews itself, as expressed in the morning liturgy: "In God's goodness, He renews daily, perpetually, the work of creation." How did spiritual entities (worlds two and three) appear if they were not already in existence in the initial, purely physical stage of the world? This problem does not exist in the Bible. The Bible records the presence of the divine spirit from the first moments of creation, and throughout the development of the world and humanity.

According to Genesis 2:7, God made man "a living being" by breathing the "soul of life" into his nostrils: "And the Lord God created man from the dust of the earth and filled his nostrils with the soul of life and man became a living being." God breathed the *soul* into man's already existing body. The soul came to man from outside, so according to the Torah's view, the body and soul are separate, independent entities, blending into one another through God's action. Moreover, the Torah states that the source of the soul is God. As R. Joseph B. Soloveitchik (a leading twentieth-century authority on Jewish law and philosopher of Judaism) writes: "Man was created in the image of God. A spark of creation was concealed within him" ("*U-bikashtem mi-sham*," 154).

The sages derive the following fundamental principle from the Torah:

> A human has three partners: God, his father, and his mother. His father gives the white from which come the bones and tendons... His mother gives redness from which develop skin and flesh... God gives him spirit and soul, wisdom and intelligence, and when the time comes to leave this world, God removes his part, and leaves the father's and mother's parts. (Tractate Niddah 31a)

The kabbalists agree that the soul and all its parts are a spiritual unit whose source is in the upper worlds and in the divine lordship that trickles down and attaches itself to the body for the fulfillment of a particular function.

The source of the soul in the Jewish tradition is God. Yet not only is the source of the soul divine, but the necessary connection between man and the divine exists, permanently and temporarily. "The intellect that overflowed from Him toward us is the bond between us and Him. You have the choice: if you wish to strengthen and to fortify this bond [with the divine intellect] you can do so; if, however, you wish gradually to make it weaker and feebler until you cut it, you can also do that" (Maimonides, *Guide of the Perplexed* 3:51).

The Bible records a plethora of testimonials of relationships between humanity and the divine, between human souls and the divine. Particularly impressive is the story of the initial contact between Samuel and the divine as described in I Samuel 3:4–8:

> God called to Samuel, and he said, "Here I am." He ran to Eli and said, "Here I am, for you called me." But he said, "I did not call; go back and lie down," so he went and lay down. God continued to call again, "Samuel!" so Samuel arose and went to Eli and said, "Here I am, for you called me." But he said, "I did not call, my son. Go back and lie down." Samuel had not yet known God, and the word of God had not yet been revealed to him. God continued to call, "Samuel!" a third time, and he arose and went to Eli and said, "Here I am, for you called me." Then Eli realized that God was calling the lad.

The Bible methodically cites testimony describing the relationship between man and the divine. (Biblical criticism completely ignores this relationship. The failure to acknowledge it is an a priori assumption superimposed onto reality with no basis in logic or in reality.) Of course, direct communication between humans and the divine has existed throughout history, not only in biblical times. Divine revelation filled the Jew's world three. It represents the most significant part of that world, as well as the world three of all humanity. The Jew's inner world, his world two anchored in the Jewish world three, is the basis upon which he builds his spiritual life and develops his ability to communicate with the divine. The actualization of this ability is a religious experience and is dependent on his spiritual efforts.

According to Popper, world three is man-made. This does not contradict human reception of new knowledge through divine revelation. Man only transfers the message to world three, filling world three with messages from an outside source. From this perspective, world three remains autonomous. It is independent of human beings and their construction of it. In chapter 4, section 8, which discusses history, we will outline the concept of the universe comprising these three worlds (one, two, and three) and open to divine providence.

8. Summary

For the duration of our lives we deal with two opposing tendencies: materialistic versus spiritual-religious. Apparently, all of our accumulated experience is testimony to the validity of the materialist tendency. A child's first creative work is a house constructed from blocks. The cars whizzing around on our streets and highways are made of material parts. The most sophisticated computers are formed from material components. Human beings are the most complex mechanisms in the world. Our organs and brains are made of materials. But scientific study may be the most convincing evidence for materialism. We have already mentioned the incredible achievements made by science in the modern era.

Neither the basic assumptions nor the results of scientific study include the mind. On the other hand, from childhood and throughout my entire life I have felt and experienced my self. I feel my self directly, without mediation. I need no proof—logical or experimental—of the existence of my self. Renowned twentieth-century philosopher Bertrand Russell asserted: "I hold...that whatever we know without inference is mental" (*Human Knowledge: Its Scope and Limits*, 240).

I perceive the external world through my intellect, through my self. The reality of self is primary for me. This is not a metaphysical-philosophical claim, but rather a fact of my life. My consciousness perceives everything that takes place in the world, be it in my personal life, or that of my family or friends, as part of the reality of my self. There are times when I am not fully conscious, e.g., when asleep or under general anesthesia during surgery, and when I awaken and find my self unchanged, I come to the conclusion that my self has continuity. My child-self and my adult-self are one and the same. I have no doubt whatsoever regarding the reality of my self.

I will expand on this topic in a more general direction. The world is so complex that human beings cannot understand it completely. When humans reach the limits of their understanding and perceive these limits, they approach profundity. True understanding is to stand on the brink of things that we have no capability of comprehending. As the Psalmist writes: "How great are your deeds, Lord, exceedingly profound are your thoughts. A simple man cannot know, nor can a fool understand this" (Psalms 92:7–8). However, this does not mean that a wise and clever person does understand God's thoughts and the greatness of His deeds. Rather, the psalm says that a wise person "will understand *this*"—exactly how great are God's deeds and how deep his thoughts, though the person is incapable of understanding those thoughts and deeds.

For those who remain unimpressed by the words in Psalms, I refer to Albert Einstein's observation that "[the scientist's] religious feeling takes the form of a rapturous amazement at the harmony of natural law, which reveals an intelligence of such superiority that, compared with it, all the systematic thinking and acting of human beings is an utterly insignificant reflection" (*Ideas and Opinions*, 50).

I return now to the dilemma at hand. We accustom ourselves to routine in our daily lives, and as a result of these habits, we do not see one of the greatest miracles in the world, if not the greatest. This miracle is the self, our own self and that of every person on the planet. Humans are foreign objects in the physical world. Humanity's appearance on the planet could not have been predicted according to the laws of physics. Furthermore, science cannot explain the phenomenon of the appearance of humanity in the time frame given. Science can describe or explain to some degree all the material parts comprising human organs, including the most complex organ, the brain. But the self is not comprised of material parts, nor is its behavior determined by physical or chemical laws only.

The awareness that I am composed of two entities, material and spiritual, is not easy, if possible at all. Maybe this is the threshold between the understandable and the inconceivable discussed above. We have difficulty categorizing an everyday experience as wondrous. As an example, consider a child accustomed to television who sees nothing strange about it. This child must mature and learn a great deal in order to understand how a television works. This example is limited in that a television can be understood through science, while my inner world, my self, cannot.

We must make an enormous mental effort in order to overcome the childish approach that takes everyday experiences for granted. Above we used examples of machines such as automobiles and computers. The common thread in these examples is that a human must always operate these machines. Biologists study the human brain and conclude that perhaps the brain is a sophisticated computer, the most sophisticated kind. But no machine or computer runs on its own. Someone must navigate the car or plane, someone needs to program the computer, operate it, and read its data output. Here we reach a critical point requiring intellectual endeavor to detach from ordinary thinking. My brain has a master, who programs and operates it, and that master is the self. The mystery is that I have no tools to describe the self and the way it operates the body and the brain.

We have become accustomed to the ability of science to describe everything, including machines and biological organs. We are used to the idea that everything is composed of material. But here we must leave our routine way of thinking and begin to understand that there is mystery here. My spiritual self utilizes the brain as its personal computer. The authors of *The Self and Its Brain* do not touch upon this mystery. They accept as fact that the mind works the brain and directs the entire body. How? The authors intentionally avoid such questions. Modern physics also suffices with the symbolic language of mathematical equations without getting into the essence of things, nor does it purport to do so. In other words, something non-biological (non-material) does exist, and that is the self, which "uses" the human body and brain.

Identification of the spiritual self opens the door to faith. As for the Jewish perspective, according to R. Soloveitchik's statement above, each of us has the divine spark within. Centuries ago, Maimonides pointed out:

> Man possesses as his proprium [nature] something in him that is very strange as it is not found in anything else that exists under the sphere of the moon, namely, intellectual apprehension.... It was because of this something, I mean *because of the divine intellect conjoined with man*, that it is said of the latter that he is "in the image of God and in His likeness." (*Guide of the Perplexed* 1:1; emphasis mine)

The bond between man and God is continuous, at least as a possibility, but men have the God-given right to freedom of choice. We can reinforce or weaken this bond (ibid. 3:51) (see section 7 above). Faith is the essential component for the existence of the human relationship with God.

The spiritual world of the believing Jew is based on more than the direct, personal bond between individual Jews and God. Divine contact with the people of Israel during the course of history (e.g., Mount Sinai, the parting of the Red Sea) are the basis of Jewish experience. In this regard, we can begin to understand Judaism's powerful emphasis on studying divine revelation, the Torah. This is the Jewish version of world three. Karl Popper's secular approach sees world three as strictly man-made. In contrast, in the Jewish world three, the Torah records the objective relationship between humanity and God, which existed in history.

We will go on to a fuller discussion of evolution and Darwinism in chapter 3, but one point is especially relevant here. Darwinistic evolution is material evolution, based on the inheritance of material, genes, and DNA. Evolutionary theory does not include the soul. DNA does not determine the self. Genetically identical twins are different entities, different selves.

Once R. Soloveitchik had a discussion with an evolutionary biologist. Responding to the scientist's query as to why Judaism could not accept Darwinism, the rabbi made one simple statement: he believed that man was endowed with a soul (*Tradition* 29:3, p.88).

Chapter Two

Science

1. Introduction

Many people, especially lay people, see science as a barrier to religion. They talk about the scientific worldview, and claim that science has proved the truth of atheism. They think science explains life on earth and differentiation of the species. They even claim that science explains the phenomenon of the soul, if they do not completely negate its existence. In short, this worldview holds that science explains everything, leaving no room for religion and faith. In this chapter I will show that this approach has no basis. Still, many support this view, and it has had a destructive influence on faith and religion. Probably for this reason, one stream of Judaism has distanced itself greatly from the world of science.

Thus, two completely opposing sectors, because of their superficial knowledge of science and its structure, have arrived at the same false conclusion—that science and religion cannot coexist. In this context, we may cite findings from many locations around the globe: there are more believers among researchers in the exact sciences than among those in the humanities. In my opinion, the explanation is simple. Those who work in the exact sciences are aware of their limitations and assumptions, whereas many of those in the humanistic disciplines receive their scientific knowledge secondhand.

Science's validity and authority stem from its incredible achievements in the modern age. The late Yeshayahu Leibowitz wrote in his book *Conversations about Science and Values* that the very existence of the human race today depends upon the advancement of science. For approximately two hundred years, man has been surrounded by a world created by science. For example, we rarely use raw, natural materials. As a result of scientific advancements, from the middle of the eighteenth century until today—about twelve generations—the earth's population has grown about sevenfold. This rate is enormous compared to the previous two thousand years, when the population only doubled.

We will discuss here what used to be called "the natural sciences"—physics, chemistry, and biology. Physics is the foundation of the natural sciences. Mathematics has a special relationship with the natural sciences, but is not included within them. The basis of science is theoretical science, characterized by basic rules called "the laws of nature." On this topic, we confront such challenging questions as what is the source of man's knowledge, and how can man understand the laws of nature? Although these questions may not seem particularly difficult, the problem of the source of scientific cognition is one of the most fundamental and difficult, both in general philosophy and in Jewish thought.

Man's ability to obtain knowledge, develop theories, and discover the laws of nature is a miracle from the viewpoint of secular philosophy as well as that of science. We have already seen this phenomenon above (1.8) when we showed that often laymen are not capable of understanding the depth of a problem. On the other hand, even when a wise person understands the depth of the problem, he is not always capable of solving it. Karl Popper, who was preeminent in the field of the philosophy of science, writes, "The phenomenon of human knowledge is no doubt the greatest miracle in our universe" (*Objective Knowledge*, vii). Albert Einstein expresses himself similarly: "The eternal mystery of the world is its comprehensibility.... The fact that it is comprehensible is a miracle" (*Ideas and Opinions*, 285). R. Soloveitchik is also aware of this problem: "The process of cognition, the problem of problems and enigma of enigmas of man, reveals itself in all its splendor and majesty" (*Halakhic Man*, 8).

In this chapter we will endeavor to understand science, its structure, and source. As soon as we understand why scientific cognition is a miracle (from a "scientific" point of view), this will lead us to comprehend the structure of science and its limitations. Therefore, we will now focus on the problem of *scientific cognition*.

2. *The Principle of Induction*

How is it possible to know the world? A central field in philosophy deals with this question: the theory of cognition, or *epistemology*. Most people do not see any difficulty in the question of scientific cognition. They think we can infer scientific theories and the laws of nature from experiment and observation.

We recognize the world through our five senses, using experimental data and rational thought to formulate laws of nature. This approach, from the particular to the general, is called *induction*. The opposite process of reaching conclusions from the general to the particular is called *deduction*. The basis of induction is the principle that we can infer the general, in this case the laws of nature and scientific theories, from the particular, meaning experimental results and observations.

Research scientists are not always experts in the theory of cognition, and in general believe in induction. Moreover, Bertrand Russell, one of the most important philosophers of the twentieth century, asserted that science could not discover the laws of nature without the principle of induction. At first glance, the principle of induction fits our commonsense view of the world.

Yet in the eighteenth century, the Scottish philosopher David Hume proved that the principle of induction has no validity and is erroneous. In his book *Treatise of Human Nature*, he proves that it is impossible to infer laws of nature based on experiments. In his opinion, induction has no substance, and no logical argument can prove that "the incidents about which we have no experience are similar to those for which we have experience." This means that "even observation of a regular or fixed combination of objects cannot infer anything about any object beyond our experience." In other words, *we can infer no theory from experience.* This means that we cannot construct theories in a rational way, using logical processes, and based on observable data alone.

We can illustrate this with an analogy from mathematics. Let us take a given numerical series. We will ask ourselves if it is possible to infer any conclusion about it based on knowledge of part of it, even a large part. For instance, if we know a small part of the series is 1,2,3,4, what can we say about the whole series based on this partial knowledge? It is possible that this is a series of natural numbers: 1,2,3,4,5,6,7,8,9,10,... However, it could also be part of a series of numbers such as: 1,2,3,4 1,2,3,4 1,2,3,4. Even more detailed knowledge, such as 1,2,3,4,1,2,3,4, still does not necessarily indicate a specific known series. The series could be, for example, 1,2,3,4 1,2,3,4 4,3,2,1 4,3,2,1. The possibilities are infinite. Based on the knowledge of a limited section, we cannot infer any conclusion about a certain sequence of numbers.

Karl Popper studied David Hume's writings regarding the principle of induction. Based on Hume's ideas, Popper formulated a formal proof negating induction. His proof is based on the fact that a number of past observations and a possible future observation, such as a solar eclipse, constitute a consistent framework of observations.

The law of induction contradicts simple logic. If this law were correct, then any theory based on a certain group of past experiments will determine the results of all experiments, past and future. As a result, *limited* knowledge based on a group of past experiments determines the results of an *infinite* number of past and future experiments. This is the essence of the law of induction. It has no proof; it is only an assumption that has no logical foundation. In our example above of the infinite series of numbers, the principle of induction determines the *entire* series on the basis of limited knowledge about certain numbers.

A formal proof of the invalidity of the induction principle

The following is a restatement of Karl Popper's proof (itself a restatement of David Hume's critique of inductive reasoning) found in *Conjectures and Refutations* (pages 189–190).

Let us consider class K of statements based on past observations of actual events that we know to be true, and furthermore to be consistent with each other.

Now let us consider a self-consistent statement B, which represents a logically possible future observation, an event that might logically occur. For example, statement B might be that a solar eclipse will be observed tomorrow. Since solar eclipses have been observed in the past, this statement is logically possible and therefore self-consistent—it does not contradict itself.

Hume explains that if B represents a logically possible future observation, and K is a group of genuine assertions about past results of observations, then we can add B to K without a logical contradiction. *No logically possible future observation can ever contradict a group of observations carried out in the past*.

Now, according to logical principles, if B can be added to K, then B can also be added to any statements that are derived from K, which will also be self-consistent. A logically possible future event B, then, will not contradict statements derived from class K of past observations.

If Newton's theory could be arrived at by inductive reasoning—that is, derived from class K of actual past events—then no statement B about a logically possible future event could contradict Newton's theory.

Newton's theory, which explains gravitational pull and thus can be used to make statements about the orbits of the planets and heavenly bodies, allows us to make predictions about whether or not a solar eclipse will actually take place on a given day.

So let us assume that through calculations based on Newton's theory, we are able to state that there will in fact not be an eclipse tomorrow. Our statement B, which did not contradict class K of past observations, and therefore should have been consistent with any statement derived from past observations (in this case, Newton's theory), is now inconsistent.

We see therefore that Newton's theory cannot be derived from class K of observed past events.

The example of the series relies on the hidden assumption of a certain order in the numbers, and this is a simplified assumption that does not necessarily reflect reality. The results of a certain number of experiments do not enable us to determine the results of all subsequent experiments, nor do they allow us to determine a certain order in the future reality. In any case, such a conclusion does not stem from the results of our experiments, and does not depend on the number of experiments carried out. *In a rational way, on the basis of logical reasoning, we cannot infer scientific theories from experiments.*

The negation of the law of induction places a serious problem squarely on the doorstep of the scientific law of cognition. How can we formulate laws of nature if not by inference from the findings of observations? Bertrand Russell expresses his opinion about this in a picturesque way. According to Russell, David Hume "arrives at the disastrous conclusion that from experience and observation nothing is to be learnt. There is no such thing as a rational belief.... The lunatic who believes that he is a poached egg is to be condemned solely on the grounds that he is in the minority.... This is a desperate point of view, and it must be hoped that there is some way of escaping from it" (*A History of Western Philosophy*, 672).

Karl Popper called this the *problem of induction*. He claimed to have solved it, as far as this is possible within the framework of secular thinking—i.e., a framework that does not recognize a spirit beyond life or outside of man. But Immanuel Kant, who preceded Popper, had already suggested a solution of his own. We will describe his solution in section 4 below.

3. Gödel's Theorem

David Hume proved that man is not capable of inferring the laws of nature *by induction from the particular to the general*, on the basis of experimental findings and logical reasoning. Is the situation different in mathematics? Here we are in the realm of pure logic, and one might suppose that we could infer mathematical assertions in a logical fashion from other assertions. This means that laws could be inferred from certain basic premises, from the general to the particular, which is *deduction*, not *induction*. We gain the impression that we can establish all mathematical knowledge on a solid foundation, inferring mathematical truths through logical and rational actions, in algorithms. The algorithm is a finite series of logical actions that are well defined. In computer language, an algorithm is a finite, logical series of commands contained in a certain program.

David Hilbert, an important early twentieth-century mathematician, assumed that all mathematical truths could be deduced in algorithms from a certain number of axioms. He did not prove his assumption, and in fact left it as an unsolved problem. If this assumption is correct, and we can write a procedure for solving mathematical problems with algorithms, then a sophisticated computer, as well as the world's most sophisticated computer—that is, the human brain—should be able to solve all mathematical problems.

Hilbert's program, an algorithmic structure of all mathematics, failed when the brilliant Austrian mathematician Kurt Gödel proved his remarkable theorem, known as "Gödel's theorem." Gödel answered Hilbert's question: in principle, does a procedure exist by which we can solve all mathematical problems, one after the other? Gödel proved the answer is negative.

Gödel's theorem asserts that in every mathematical system of axioms and rules for proving theorems, there are statements that cannot be proved or negated (proved incorrect).

His only underlying assumption is that the system has a minimum number of arithmetic rules or laws. Thus, for example, geometry (Euclidean and non-Euclidean), in its classic formulation, includes no arithmetic, and therefore Gödel's theorem does not apply to it. On the other hand, analytical geometry uses algebraic and analytic methods, describing geometrical concepts in numbers. Therefore Gödel's theorem applies to analytical geometry.

Gödel proved that certain mathematical truths cannot be derived through algorithmic operations. In fact, Kurt Gödel arrived at a conclusion similar to Hume's. He proved that even in the domain of abstract mathematics, logical and algorithmic operations are not sufficient to derive all mathematical truths.

4. *Immanuel Kant's Solution to the Problem of Induction*

Immanuel Kant, like most of his enlightened generation in the eighteenth century, believed that Newton's mechanics was absolute truth. Therefore he had to confront the question of how to prove this theory *on the basis of experimental findings*, when David Hume had proved that it was impossible. The question that Kant asked himself was: how was science (i.e., Newton's mechanics) possible?

It took a long time for Kant to arrive at what he thought was the solution. His solution seemed to be original and innovative, even revolutionary, and difficult to understand. In the future, philosophers of science would make significant changes in this solution (see Popper, in the next section), but Immanuel Kant made a breakthrough in the doctrine of scientific cognition. Accordingly, we will find it worthwhile to strain our minds in order to grasp the essence of his solution, even if we cannot comprehend it completely.

Kant's idea was that human intelligence conceives of laws and imposes them on the raw material of the experiment. Man arrives at these laws a priori, before the experiment, and without connection to the experiment. We use these a priori laws to organize the raw data of the experiment. These laws are claims—general, universal statements that we impose on the world of the experiment. Euclidean space and time are a priori categories of this kind. In Kant's opinion, these categories are not derived from any experiment, but are functions and rules of human intelligence that allow us to organize the findings of our experience. This claim about the geometry of space is not self-evident, as we might assume. In fact, the German mathematician Carl Friedrich Gauss (1777–1855) already noted that the Euclidean nature of space can be observed through experiments, and he even tried to do so. Einstein's general theory of relativity clarified the dependence of spatial geometry on the matter present in space.

David Hume proved that we cannot rationally infer the principle of causality from experience. In contrast, Immanuel Kant asserted the existence of an a priori statement that determines that every event has its own cause. (Indeed, the alleged possibility of deducing the causality, that every event has its cause, from the experiment is a specific case of the induction principle.) "In order to test Hume's problematical concept [his *crux metaphysicorum*], the concept of cause, we are first given a priori, by means of logic, the form of a conditional judgment in general; that is, we have one cognition given as antecedent and another as consequent" (*Prolegomena to Any Future Metaphysics*, 59). Kant suggests that the very existence of laws connecting the cause and the effect (causality) could be established on an a priori basis. The same is true for the laws themselves—they cannot be deduced from the experiments, but could be established on an a priori basis.

This was a breakthrough in philosophy in general, and specifically in the philosophy of scientific awareness: human intellect plays an active part in the establishment of the laws of nature. Kant called his theory the "Copernican Revolution." Men are not just instruments that process data entering from the outside world. In modern parlance we may describe it like this: the most sophisticated of computers would not be able to formulate laws of nature, even if it had all possible data (David Hume's claim), but human reason is capable of this (Kant's claim).

Immanuel Kant's primary contribution was his discovery of the role of human reason in the process of scientific cognition. However, several questions remain open. *How* does human reason obtain this a priori knowledge? Is this knowledge indisputable? The answer that Kant suggested to the latter question stemmed from his belief that physics was an absolute science, absolute truth. Accordingly, the a priori knowledge is also unequivocally true. As to the first question, it remains open.

Let us examine this first question: How does human reason obtain the a priori knowledge that we use to organize our experiences?

Immanuel Kant distinguished between two types of a priori statements: *analytic* a priori, and *synthetic* a priori. Kant defines the *analytic* statement as one that elucidates yet does not add to prior knowledge. This knowledge logically stems from what was known previously. On the other hand, *synthetic* a priori statements add to existing knowledge. In other words, the *synthetic* statement constitutes *new knowledge*. The assumption "a tall man is a man" is an analytic claim derived from the law of contrast and contradiction, since the premise "a tall man is not a man" includes an unsustainable contradiction. In contradistinction, every statement known to us from experience is synthetic. We cannot arrive at statements such as "yesterday was a rainy day" (a synthetic claim) by the analysis of concepts alone.

Clearly, scientific theories and laws of nature are synthetic statements, and constitute new knowledge. Kant's theory relates to *synthetic* a priori statements that man can discover with his intelligence. How can this be? Kant does not have an answer to this, although he writes about it prolifically, calling it a "transcendental" method: the method of taking scientific knowledge as a fact, and seeking to discover the principles which would explain how this fact was possible.

David Hume's philosophical discovery, the negation of the principle of induction, poses a serious challenge for human thought. It takes us to the outer boundaries of our understanding as human beings, the same border that we described above (1.8).

Immanuel Kant's solution was an important step in the comprehension of scientific cognition, but not all philosophers agreed with him. I have already mentioned Bertrand Russell's opinion, which diverged from Kant's solution. He tried to salvage the principle of induction. In his opinion, science cannot exist at all without this principle: "If this principle [induction] is not true, every attempt to arrive at general scientific laws from particular observations is fallacious..." (*A History of Western Philosophy*, 674). However, Russell's solution was not fundamentally different from Kant's. Russell assumed that induction itself constitutes an independent logical principle that cannot be inferred from experience or from other logical principles. He asserts, "without this principle science is impossible" (ibid.). Russell assumed here that the principle of induction is a *synthetic* a priori statement. His claim is not significantly different from Kant's assertion that the principle of causality is a *synthetic* a priori claim.

Here we note a certain reservation. Ordinary scientific reasoning is based on logic, on deductive inference of conclusions, from the general to the particular. Science follows rules of deductive inference. However, science has no rules governing inductive inference. We can say, at most, on the basis of induction, that it seems that the future will not be much different from the past. This rule is so vague that it cannot provide the basis for scientific inquiry.

Kant's theory "is a strange mixture of absurdity and truth" (Popper, *Conjectures and Refutations*, 95). It tried to prove something that could not be proved—the absolute truth of Newton's theory. But his attempt took us in the right direction: people are the creators of scientific theories.

5. *Karl Popper's Solution to the Problem of Induction*

Now we will approach Karl Popper's solution to the problem of induction. As we explained, the problem of induction is central to the theory of scientific cognition. We may present the problem in the following way: On the one hand, David Hume proved that based on data from experiment or observation, we cannot infer any theory or law of nature. On the other hand, man does indeed discover scientific theories and laws of nature. How, or on what basis, can we derive the laws of nature, if not from experience?

Karl Popper suggests a solution to the problem of induction in his monographs: *Logik der Forschung* (*The Logic of Scientific Discovery*), the aforementioned *Conjectures and Refutations*, *Objective Knowledge*, and *Unended Quest*. Here we will try to condense his theory of scientific cognition into a few sentences. Popper replaced inductive methodology—which tries to obtain scientific laws from observation and infers from the *particular* to the *general*—with deductive methodology, which infers from the *general* to the *particular*. In Popper's opinion, science is not inductive, as "induction was a myth that David Hume smashed." *We must view all laws and theories as hypotheses, or assumptions (i.e., guesses).* These theories are the work of men. They are fundamental assumptions that cannot be inferred from experience or observation. Accordingly, *the structure of science became deductive—from the general to the particular.*

Both Kant and Popper agree that science is deductive. Both Kant and Popper agree that people are the creators of scientific theories. The difference between them is this: According to Kant, theories are based on *absolute* a priori categories (not derived from experience). Popper, on the other hand, assumes that theories are only *hypotheses*, or *guesses*. This difference stems, in fact, from the revolution that shook physics after the publication of Einstein's theory of relativity. Kant saw Newton's mechanics and his theory of gravity as absolute truths. Therefore, Kant was committed to absolute a priori categories and terms. After the publication of Einstein's special and general theories of relativity and after the introduction of quantum theory, scientists ceased to consider physics theories absolute.

New theories negate previous theories. Even in modern physics, theories such as Einstein's are only hypotheses or guesses. Einstein himself agrees with this point of view. "The concepts which arise in our thought and in linguistic expressions are all—when viewed logically—the free creations of thought which cannot inductively be gained from sense experiences. This is not so easily noticed only because we have the habit of combining certain concepts and conceptual relations (propositions) so definitely with certain sense experiences that we do not become conscious of the gulf—*logically unbridgeable*—which separates the world of sensory experiences from the world of concepts and propositions" (*Ideas and Opinions*, 33; emphasis mine).

Later Einstein adds: "The supreme task of the physicist is to arrive at those universal elementary laws from which the cosmos can be built up by pure deduction. There is no logical path to these laws" (ibid., 221). Einstein supports Popper in recognizing that *scientific theory is a free creation of human thought*: it is all a hypothesis or guess. If so, we might ask, are there any rational or experimental arguments that give preference to one hypothesis over the other?

Karl Popper's answer is as follows: no hypotheses and no guesses (i.e., scientific theories) can be verified by experiment. In order to verify a theory, one must perform an infinite number of experiments, including future experiments, which is impossible in principle. A great number of experiments can only corroborate scientific theory, but cannot verify it, or prove its truth. The results of many experiments have matched (or did not contradict) Newton's mechanics and theory of gravity. Over a long period of time, the vast majority of scientists and philosophers were convinced that Newton's theory was proven as absolute truth. Whoever dared to doubt Newton's theory was considered a heretic.

Solomon Maimon, who lived almost a hundred years after Newton, was such a skeptic (more about him below). When Maimon asserted that Newton's theory was a hypothesis, the earth trembled. Kant could not compete with Maimon, and in a private letter, described him as a parasite, like all Jews. "When a universalist such as Kant speaks disparagingly towards someone connected to a certain group, we can assume that he knows that he is in intellectual distress, as he is not speaking honestly" (Agassi, *The History of the New Philosophy*, 278).

Thus, according to Popper, verification of any theory (or guess) is impossible. The only acceptable method is *to prefer one hypothesis to another by refuting one of them*. Refuting a theory is possible by disproving (theoretically, or empirically, i.e., experimentally) the deductive consequences of the theory, which we have obtained by logical inference. Therefore, a handful of experiments, or even one, that contradicts the theory is sufficient. To Popper, scientific theories remain hypotheses until they are refuted.

Of course, we are eager to know the truth, to discover "true" theories. However, as we explained above, we cannot verify any theory through experiments. With regard to experimental proof, verification and refutation are not equivalent processes since they are asymmetrical. In order to refute a theory, we have only to carry out one experiment that contradicts a deductive consequence of the theory. In other words, "*All theories are hypotheses*; all *may* be overthrown" (Popper, *Objective Knowledge*, 29).

In a certain sense, Popper's theory of scientific cognition is an outcome of Einstein's revolution in science. Einstein's theory refuted Newton's theory and left to it only a limited realm of application. After Einstein, there was no room for compulsive commitment to unequivocal proof of a certain theory. Theories are free creations of human thought; however, human intellect need not impose its creation on nature. On the contrary, Popper writes that "we question nature, as Kant taught us to do; and we try to elicit from her *negative* answers concerning the truth of our theories: we do not try to prove or to *verify* them, but we test them by trying to *disprove* or to falsify them, to *refute* them" (*Conjectures and Refutations*, 192).

Popper bases his solution to the problem of scientific cognition on hypotheses, guesses that scientists who are in the category of geniuses may discover. These hypotheses are not necessarily correct. Possibly, even quite probably, one day new theories will replace them; they too will be hypotheses that will remain in the realm of guesses.

6. *Man's Ability to Reveal Nature's Laws*

We have not yet approached the essence of the problem of scientific cognition. From our point of view, the essence of the problem is man's ability to discover the laws of nature. Karl Popper does not even pretend to deal with this problem. Furthermore, analysis of the significance of scientific cognition brings him, paradoxically, to the conclusion that this problem is insolvable. "[E]ven on the assumption...that our quest for knowledge has been very successful so far, and that we now know something of our universe, this success becomes miraculously improbable, and therefore inexplicable; for an appeal to an endless series of improbable accidents is not an explanation" (*Objective Knowledge*, 28).

No theory can explain the success of our search for the laws of nature: "Successful explanation must retain, on any valid theory, the probability zero, assuming that we measure this probability, approximately, by the ratio of the 'successful' explanatory hypotheses to all hypotheses which might be designed by man" (Popper, *Conjectures and Refutations*, 96).

We are touching upon a most important point and return to Albert Einstein who insisted that "there is no logical path to these laws [of physics].... [O]ut of all conceivable constructions, a single one has always proved itself decidedly superior to all the rest" (*Ideas and Opinions*, 221).

Following are the testimonies of two other distinguished scientists—E. P. Wigner and R. Penrose—who have addressed these issues:

> The real physical world seems to accord in a remarkable way with some very precise mathematical schemes.... It has often been remarked how extraordinary this precision actually is (cf. especially Wigner 1960 ["The Unreasonable Effectiveness of Mathematics," *Communications on Pure and Applied Mathematics* 13 (1960): 1–14]). It is hard for me to believe, as some have tried to maintain, that such SUPERB theories could have arisen merely by some random natural selection of ideas leaving only the good ones as survivors. The good ones are simply much *too* good to be the survivors of ideas that have arisen in that random way." (Penrose, *The Emperor's New Mind*, 556)

As we saw, Popper considered all theories merely hypotheses. The Einsteinian revolution relegated not only Newton's theory, but also all theories of physics to the realm of hypotheses. "The quest for certainty, for a secure basis of knowledge, has to be abandoned" (*Objective Knowledge*, 37).

We are now capable of understanding the logic of scientific cognition—a priori hypotheses, their refutation, new hypotheses, and so on, ad infinitum. However, the central problem of scientific cognition, the source of these hypotheses, lies outside this logic. The atheistic method we have described, which ignores interaction with the infinite mind, comes to the paradoxical conclusion that *men are not capable of producing a scientific discovery*. To use scientific terminology, the probability of finding a suitable hypothesis is zero.

In order to show that this claim is not merely an abstract philosophical one, I will offer two examples of "suitable" hypotheses. The findings of modern physics are not tangible; we cannot visualize them—that is, perceive them with our senses—as we can statements of classical physics. We can illustrate Newton's theory of gravity by pointing to an apple falling from a tree. In Einstein's theory of gravity (the theory of general relativity), movement in the gravitational field is described by a geodesic line in curved four-dimensional space-time. Quantum theory is even more abstract. Physical quantities such as coordinates (place), momentum, and energy are described using very abstract mathematical concepts that have no direct connection with our sensory experiences. There is no point in even trying to explain them.

In short, the physical theory, a conjecture, is not something that has a close resemblance to the observed phenomenon. Physicists formulate theories in such abstract terms that most people are barely capable of grasping them at all.

From a logical point of view, the creation of a new, fundamental theory is creation *ex nihilo*. Before Einstein formulated his theory of relativity, this theory did not exist. We cannot logically infer it from another previously existing concept or theory. Einstein did not create it from already existing material or ideas, or as a logical continuation to them. In other words, basic theories such as Newton's mechanics, Einstein's theory of relativity, and the quantum theory are new creations. They were created *ex nihilo*.

In the above analysis, we have not discussed the connection between man and his Creator. In chapter 1, we already wrote that *ex nihilo* means openness of the world, and man in it, to God. Through this, we arrive at the Jewish concept of the problem of scientific cognition.

7. Scientific Cognition in the Real World—A Jewish View

Until now, we have spoken about the abstract world of philosophers, the fruits of an effort to reconstruct the world without divinity. To recall the analogy we used previously (1.6), this is like trying to explain a physical world while knowing nothing about light. The creation of the world, from the point of view of physics, is a creation from absolute nothingness, *ex nihilo*. This parallels Maimonides' outlook (*Guide of the Perplexed* 2:3) and other Jewish sources, but these sources also include another significant component—God.

We learn about the Jewish view of understanding the world from the first report on creation in the book of Genesis. As stated in Ethics of the Fathers, "With ten utterances the world was created" (1:5).

What does this teach us? The Torah relates that the world was created in ten pronouncements, in order to teach us that this world has meaning, and we depend on God's will, on His revelation to us, in order to teach us something about the meaning of the world.

The source of our knowledge of reality is God's word and thought. The combination of the words "was created" and "with utterances" implies the potential for understanding. The *word* itself turns into reality ("God said, 'Let there be light,' and there was light" [Genesis 1:3]), implying that the reality is rational: it is based on the *word*. This means also that the very essence of reality can be understood in principle, though the fulfillment of our comprehension of the world depends upon God's will. Reality is both rational and intelligible. In the Torah, the process of creation means the appearance of order among chaos. God created order and lawfulness.

Now, what are the alternatives to this Jewish approach that sees the source of reality in God, in His pronouncement? A materialist approach sees the material as the source of everything. If this is so, there is no reason that the world should be comprehensible to us, and there is also no reason that there should be order, or any reason that it should be rational.

A more moderate dualistic *secular* approach, that of Popper's three worlds theory, also fails to solve the problem of scientific cognition and the comprehensibility of the world, as we saw above. The world is comprised of three worlds: the world of the material (world one), the inner world of man (world two), and the world of objective knowledge, which is the product of man (world three). *The possibility of a new creation, ex nihilo, is not inherent in this world lacking divinity.* If it is indeed possible, then it constitutes a miracle (creation *ex nihilo*), in complete contradiction to the secular approach.

I conclude that for understanding how it came to be that the world is comprehensible, the various secular approaches offer no reasonable alternative to Judaism.

The only thing that was created on the first day is the separation between light and darkness. This means that light has a special meaning in the biblical text. Light is not only a physical entity (although it has a physical aspect too): "I saw that there is an advantage to the wisdom and the folly, just as the light from the darkness" (Ecclesiastes 2:13). "A new light will shine on Zion, and we will merit its light speedily. Blessed are You, O God, the Creator of the lights" (morning liturgy). In the parables of the Jewish sages, light often signifies understanding reality.

"R. Judah says: Light was created first, then the world. This can be compared to a king who wanted to build a palace, but the area was dark. What did he do? He lit candles and torches, so as to know where to establish the foundations. Thus the light was created first" (Genesis Rabbah 3). The concept of light in biblical texts symbolizes two main ideas. First, light indicates the comprehensibility of a reality that we can research and understand. Second, light symbolizes a positive approach to reality. Here lies the source of the Bible's inherent optimism. The world originated with *utterances* and *light*, and it is a world that we are capable of understanding.

God created man and the world with the intention of a reciprocal relationship between them (Genesis 1:26). This means that God planned them in such a way that people would be able, when necessary, to discover the world. Man needs the ability to understand the world for the following reasons:

1. The very goal of scientific cognition is a creative effort suitable to man. This is because we were "fashioned in the image of God [and] blessed with … the intelligence, the human mind, capable of confronting the outside world and inquiring into its complex workings" (R. Soloveitchik, *The Lonely Man of Faith*, 12).
2. Cognition of the world allows man to control nature. "God, in imparting the blessings to Adam … and giving him the mandate to subdue nature, directed Adam's attention to the functional and practical aspects of his intellect through which man is able to gain control of nature" (ibid.).
3. Recognizing God's wisdom, courage, and kindness, and exploring His creations, brings man to love of God. Love of God is a positive commandment: "You will love the Lord your God with all your heart, and with all your soul and with all your might" (Deut. 6:5). Maimonides emphasizes that this love is a function of the understanding of the divine creation of the world (*Guide of the Perplexed* 1:39, 3:28, 3:51; *Foundations of the Torah* 2:2; *Laws of Repentance* 10:6).

Thus, the biblical worldview includes the accessibility of the world to human comprehension.

The biblical prophecy about understanding the world is gradually being fulfilled. The Psalmist recognized the greatness of the created world in his prophetic vision: "How great are Your deeds, O God, your thoughts are very deep" (Psalms 92). About three thousand years later, Newton discovered the theory of gravity and Einstein discovered his theory of relativity, the most sublime scientific theory to date. In the twentieth century, scientists discovered the quantum theory, with Einstein's fundamental contribution. This theory does not always fit our intuition, and challenges our understanding, but leads us, as Einstein put it, to a "rapturous amazement at the harmony of natural law, which reveals an intelligence of such superiority that, compared with it, all the systematic thinking and acting of human beings is an utterly insignificant reflection" (*Ideas and Opinions*, 50).

Maimonides deals extensively with the problem of intellectual achievement and awareness. In our first chapter (1.8) we already referred to his words in the *Guide of the Perplexed*:

> Man possesses as his proprium [characteristic, nature] something in him that is very strange as it is not found in anything else that exists under the sphere of the moon, namely, intellectual apprehension. In the exercise of this, no sense, no part of the body...[is] used; and therefore this apprehension was likened unto the apprehension of the deity, which does not require an instrument.... It was because of this something, I mean *because of the divine intellect conjoined with man*, that it is said of the latter that he is "in the image of God and in His likeness." (*Guide of the Perplexed* 1:1; emphasis mine)

In the previous section, we emphasized that the discovery of a new fundamental theory is similar to creation *ex nihilo*. From a secular or atheist point of view, such a new creation can be classified as a miracle, since it has no rational explanation. We saw that Einstein and Popper described this process in these terms. An important factor is missing here, like the light missing from the physical world in the parable (section 1.6). When we take God into account, we identify this missing, rational factor, for God is the reason behind the creation of the intellect. God has granted us the ability to know the world. Maimonides describes the connection between human and divine intellect in this way:

> We have already made it clear to you that that intellect which overflowed from Him...toward us is the bond between us and Him. You have the choice: if you wish to strengthen and to fortify this bond, you can do so; if, however, you wish gradually to make it weaker and feebler until you cut it, you can also do that. (*Guide of the Perplexed* 3:51)

Elsewhere, Maimonides emphasizes the connection between the creation of the world and the process of cognition: "The world derives from the overflow of God and that He has caused to overflow to it everything in it that is produced in time. In the same way it is said that He caused His knowledge to overflow to the prophets" (*Guide of the Perplexed* 2:12). Even though Maimonides emphasizes the prophetic achievement, the abundance of the infinite divine intellect is much more general and includes the process of awareness, or cognition:

> The dictum, "For with You is the fountain of life" (Psalms 36:10), signifies the overflow of being. In the same way the remaining portion of this verse, "In Thy light do we see light" has the selfsame meaning—namely, that *through the overflow of the intellect that has overflowed from Thee, we intellectually cognize, and consequently we receive correct guidance, we draw inferences, and we apprehend the intellect.* Understand this. (Ibid.; emphasis mine)

It is interesting to note that Bar-Ilan University professor Schubert Spero arrived at a similar conclusion from the *halakhic* philosophical analysis of R. Soloveitchik's writings. According to Spero, R. Soloveitchik believes "that Divinity manifests itself in human consciousness not only in rare and dramatic invasion of certain human beings by the prophetic spirit, but also in the tensions and conflicts, antinomies and polarities which are part of the general human condition" (Spero, *Tradition* 30:2, 45).

R. Abraham Y. H. Kook's writings clearly reveal this trend. In his *The Lights of Holiness* (2:3) he sees all of culture, in its various permutations, as a divine revelation:

The laws of life, laws of heaven and earth, shine with supreme light, light of greatness, light of vitality in all of existence in its highest form, wide and full, the light of everlasting life and source of all life. *All the teachings, statutes, ideas, ethics, naturalness, orders and manners, wisdoms, songs and wills,* the turbulence of life, movements of existence, its progress and grasp on the essence of being, all are but treasure houses filled with riches; the will that rises for our sake in His mighty power (*gevurah*).... (English translation in *Rav Avraham Itzhak HaCohen Kook: Between Rationalism and Mysticism,* Benjamin Ish-Shalom, 1993)

We may add R. Soloveitchik's discussion to these ideas:

God created the world as a separate and discrete entity, but did not grant it independent reality. *The world exists because it suckles from the infinite being of God....* It is a deep-rooted injustice in the haughtiness of modern man, who makes his living from cultural conquest—this is malice mixed with arrogance of the intellect that is happy with its lot in finality and temporality, and is not directed to the source of intellect. The kingship of Heaven is the kingship of true cognition, when the light of knowledge will shine on the whole universe. ("*U-bikashtem mi-sham,*" 202–203)

In Jewish thought, scientific cognition is only part of the general approach. On the one hand, as we have shown, science and secular philosophy are incapable of presenting a rational explanation for the comprehensibility of the world. According to atheist-secular philosophy, man's ability to discover the basic laws of nature is a mystery and a wonder.

In this chapter, I have been using the term "rational." Popper's definition of this term (above, 1.4) is "rational by logical principles." *Webster's Dictionary* defines the word *rational* as something that is based on *reason*.

On the other hand, one of the messages of this book is that man cannot base his outlook merely on reason. This is a naive outlook, called *rationalism*, which posits that man can understand the world *by reason alone*.

In our worldview as human beings, we must rise to a metaphysical level, whether we recognize this or not. We have to make metaphysical assumptions. This can be materialism, or secular dualism (such as Popper's), or Judaism (there are other metaphysical assumptions, but in my opinion they are less important). There are no logical, empirical proofs of one or another type of metaphysics. I think that Judaism, originating in divine revelation, is superior in status to other metaphysical theories. However, not everyone recognizes Judaism's uniqueness, and we will discuss this in the last part of the book, which deals with history.

Popper's reaction after meeting Albert Einstein was that "he [Einstein] saw clearly that there was no valid argument leading from experiment to theory; and no doubt he saw as clearly that there was no valid argument leading from science to metaphysics" (*The Open Universe*, 89). Therefore, we can identify three planes of cognition: experimental, theoretical, and metaphysical. Just as we can examine various theories and compare them, so can we examine the various types of metaphysics and compare them.

Now we will return to the term "rationalism." When we ascend to the metaphysical level of viewing the world, we seemingly ignore rationalism and the mere use of reason. For instance, the claim that the material is the source of all, including our soul, the self of each of us, does not stem from any reasoned argument. Here I arrive at an important point in this clarification. Jewish metaphysics claims that the infinite intelligence is connected to human intelligence and human reason, and from this it follows that human reason is attached to the divine infinite reason. When we say that we identify a rational explanation when we take into account a connection with God, this is rationalism in the Jewish, metaphysical sense.

In the Jewish view, human intelligence is not isolated; there is a connection between it and the infinite intelligence. Rationalism in Judaism means the wisdom of human intelligence connected to the infinite intelligence. In the Jewish metaphysical sense, the concept of rationalism has a different meaning from the reason of the isolated person, the reason of an individual without God, the reason of secular rationalism. Secular rationalism cannot explain the mere fact of a scientific discovery. In its own eyes, this is just a miracle. But in Jewish metaphysics, a scientific discovery has a rational explanation.

Popper sees materialism as irrational according to the principles of logic. Nevertheless, his *dualistic* approach does not bring rationalism into his cognition theory. According to it the comprehensibility of the world is a miracle and discoveries of all the latest fundamental theories are also miracles. In contrast with this, Judaism includes rationalism in a general picture of the world. However, this is not secular rationalism, as it includes the *ratio*, the reason of the divine infinite intelligence.

8. *Solomon Maimon and His Philosophy*

Solomon (Shlomo) Ben Yehoshua was born in the little town (shtetl) of Nieswiez, in Polish Lithuania in 1753. In his childhood, he received a traditional education in Talmud, and while still a youth, he became known as a prodigy. Wealthy Jews competed for him to marry their daughters. Thus he married at age eleven and became a father at age fourteen. He supported his family as a teacher or *melamed* in various locations, far away from home. Solomon was especially influenced by Maimonides' writings, and out of esteem for him, he called himself Solomon Maimon. He gradually became interested in pursuing secular studies, especially philosophy. He left Lithuania, and wandered through a dozen European cities.

During that time, he metamorphosed from a teacher of children in the villages of Lithuania to a renowned philosopher who corresponded with Immanuel Kant and evoked praise from him, and who influenced the German philosopher Johann Fichte. In his travels he met the Maggid of Mezritch, a pupil of the Baal Shem Tov. He became acquainted with Moses Mendelssohn, and was accepted into his circle. In 1800, Solomon was buried as an apostate outside of the Jewish cemetery in Glogau, Germany.

Between 1792 and 1793, Solomon Maimon authored his autobiography, in which he described his fascinating life. The work immediately drew attention. Below are some extracts from *The Life of Solomon Maimon.*

> Towards evening, I came to an inn and found there a Jewish beggar, who made his living in this way. I was very happy, as I had come across one of my people, with whom I could converse, and who would know these places well.
>
> I therefore decided to wander the land with my companion and to make my living in this fashion, even though it is impossible to find two people in the world who are so different from each other. I was a learned person, qualified for the rabbinate, and the other was a total ignoramus. Until then I had made an honorable living; the other was a beggar, and that was his profession. I was a person who had devoted himself to certain ideas of morality, courtesy, and politeness, and the other did not know anything of all these. Finally, my body structure was weak, although healthy enough, while the other was a strong and meaty fellow, who could have served as a choice soldier.
>
> Without heeding all these differences, I attached myself to this person, as I was forced to wander in a foreign land, in order to sustain myself. During our wanderings, I tried to provide my companion with concepts of religion and true morality, and he, on his part, taught me a chapter from the book of beggary, taught me the linguistic formulae involved in this, and even advised me in particular to curse whoever turned me away empty-handed.
>
> But with all the effort that he expended for this, I did not adopt his dogma. The formulae of begging were parasitical and blemished in my eyes.... [T]hus we wandered for half a year around the few miles of the province. In the end, we finished up on our way towards Poland.

We came to the town of Pozna, and went to the Jewish poorhouse, whose owner wore patched clothes. Here I reached the decision to end my wanderings, whatever may happen.

The autumn arrived, and the days became rather cold. I was nearly naked and barefoot. My health was affected by this path of wanderings, during which I never tasted decent food, and on the whole I was forced to make do with moldy bread crumbs and water. At night I lay on worn-out straw, sometimes even on the ground alone. Apart from this, the High Holy Days were approaching, the days of Repentance, and I, who was still quite God-fearing, could not countenance the idea of spending time in idle matters, while the rest of humanity was devoting itself to mending its ways.

Accordingly I decided not to continue in this way.... At that time I remembered that a certain rabbi from my place of birth had been accepted, a few years previously, as the rabbi of Pozna, and he had taken one of my acquaintances to serve as a scribe. I asked the youth about this friend, and I was sadly surprised to hear that he was no longer in Pozna. The rabbi had been appointed to serve in the rabbinate in Hamburg, and my friend had even gone with him there. However, he had left his son here, a boy of twelve years old, at the house of the present rabbi, who was the son-in-law of the previous rabbi....

I asked where the house of the new rabbi was, and went there, but as I was nearly naked, I was embarrassed to enter the house. I waited until I saw someone go in, and I asked him to do me a favor and call my friend's son out to me.

He immediately recognized me, and was greatly amazed when he saw my miserable situation. I told him that it was not the time to tell him of my troubles that had led me to this situation, and for now, he should just try to relieve my poverty. He promised that he would do so, and went to the rabbi and told him about me—that I was a great scholar, and God-fearing, and that special circumstances had brought me to a most grievous state of poverty.

The rabbi, who was an esteemed person, a sharp learner and of good temperament, was shaken to his foundations on hearing about my poverty. He called me to his house and talked to me for a long time, discussing important matters of study in the Talmud, and he found me expert in the subjects of the Torah.

After that, he asked me what my plans were, and I said to him that I was inquiring about obtaining a job as a teacher in one of the houses, but at that time I had no other wish than to be able to celebrate the holy festivals, and to cease my wanderings for at least those few days.

The good-hearted rabbi coaxed me to remove any worry from my heart about this and told me that what I had asked for was very little and quite fair. After that he gave me some coins, as much as he had at that time. He invited me to eat on Shabbat at his table for as long as I stayed in town, and ordered his servant to find me decent lodging. (The Life of Solomon Maimon, Part 1, chapter 22).

Maimon's wanderings and tribulations did not prevent him from completing his education, broadening his studies, and making a living as a sharp-witted philosopher. His most important composition is *Versuch uber die Transzendentalphilosophie* ("Essay on Transcendental Philosophy," 1760). Solomon Maimon said the following about this work of his:

> I wrote to Kant and sent him my composition, and also Mr. ... wrote me a letter. A long time passed with no reply. In the end the answer came, and the letter [that Kant had written] to Mr. ... said, amongst other things: "But what were you thinking of, my good friend, by sending me a large package of fine research not for reading alone, but also for study? I am sixty-six years of age, and full of much work to finish my plan (part of which is in the composition in the last part of the critique, the critique of the judicial power, which will be published very soon, and part of it in the processing of the method of metaphysics of nature and of traits in accordance with the requirements of this critique). Apart from this, an endless stream of letters occupies my attentions, which demand special clarifications

for several matters in my method, and not only this, but my health has been compromised. Accordingly, I nearly decided to send the manuscript back with an apology, which was based on the reasons above. However, I just stole a look at the manuscript, and immediately recognized its sterling worth. Not only have none of those who disagree with me understood my words and my main wish as Mr. Maimon has done, but only few have been blessed with such sharpness of intellect for such deep research, such as he.... Maimon's composition comprises such sharp comments, that if they will be published, they will certainly make a most favorable impression."

In a letter to myself, he says: "I wished to fulfill your will in as much as was possible for me, and if I was prevented from doing your will in full, and to utter a sentence about your research, you will know this reason from my letter to Mr. .... [Y]ou can rest assured that no feeling of ridicule caused me to do that, just as I do not ridicule any effort in matters of intellectual research in which humanity can find desire, all the more so in your research, out of which an unusual talent for the deeper sciences can be felt."

It is easy to understand how important and pleasant it was for me to receive the praise of this great erudite; his testimony about me, that I had understood him properly, was especially pleasing... (*The Life of Solomon Maimon*)

There are elements in Solomon Maimon's philosophy that touch upon the topic of this chapter. A careful study of Kant's writings brought Maimon to the conclusion that Kant had not solved the problem of scientific cognition. In Maimon's opinion, Kant failed in his effort to determine the real source of our a priori knowledge, assuming that it is intuition. Maimon's conclusion was that we could not arrive at the scientific cognition that we have unless our minds were part of the infinite mind:

> My opinion is therefore different from Mr. Kant's only in this—that I assume instead of...ideas that he assumes, one and only one idea

(of the infinite mind), and I attribute objective reality to this idea. Indeed, this is not when we observe it as itself (as this is against the nature of the idea), but only as far as it accepts on our part objective tangibility in different ways by objects of the observation. (*Essay on Transcendental Philosophy*, translation mine)

Accordingly, Maimon proposes his metaphysical idea in order to give scientific cognition genuine reality. The problem of the synthetic a priori assertions, which is identical to the problem of the creation of new knowledge, is thereby solved: a human being's synthetic assertion is *the infinite intelligence's own* analytical assertion. Here I remind the reader that an analytical assertion does not include new knowledge. For example, analytical statements such as "a tall man is a man" or "a triangle with three equal sides is a triangle" do not include new information. The opposite claim, "a triangle with equal sides is not a triangle," contains self-contradiction. Analytical assumptions are logical, and do not enrich the treasure trove of our knowledge.

The reality of the synthetic assertion that includes new knowledge is the foundation of scientific cognition. According to secular philosophy (like that of Popper) achievement of new knowledge, of new scientific theories, is a miraculous event, *creatio ex nihilo*; the probability of such an event is zero. Secular philosophy does not discern any real source of new knowledge. Solomon Maimon suggests that the source of this new knowledge is the infinite intelligence. For the infinite intelligence, there is no new knowledge. On the other hand, new knowledge (like knowledge of the laws of nature) is gradually revealed to man, ad infinitum. Therefore our synthetic assertions, those of mere men, are His analytical assertions. At the conclusion of his book, Solomon Maimon writes: "Our sages of the Talmud...say: 'Torah scholars do not have any rest either in this world or in the World to Come,' and as is their wont, they associate this with a verse (Psalms 84:8): 'They advance from strength to strength, the fear of God in Zion.'"

If Maimon had not left Poland, some speculate that he might have become a rabbinic luminary, and that his genius would have enriched

Judaism. If he had not spent most of his life wandering, some say, he almost certainly would have become one of the greatest philosophers of the eighteenth century (see e.g., Hebrew Encyclopedia, *Ha-Encyclopedia Ha-Ivrit*, entry "Shlomo Maimon"). In my opinion, Maimon's Jewish background, especially the legacy of Maimonides, influenced his breakthrough in the philosophy of scientific cognition, which is, in a sense, superior to that of Immanuel Kant.

9. First Conclusion: Science—Divine Revelation

The main thesis of this chapter is that the source of scientific knowledge, that is to say of the laws of nature, is divine revelation.

Popular opinion holds that experiment and observation are the basis of scientific theories about the laws of nature. To be precise, based on experimental findings, we can draw conclusions in a logical manner about scientific theories and the laws of nature. This opinion is prevalent not only among laypeople, but also among scientists who are not conversant with cognition theory. In order to understand the shakiness of this opinion it is enough only to look at a modern laboratory, which contains equipment such as mirrors, lasers, and computers (see photograph below). This is an example of a modern experiment whose purpose is to understand something about the properties of molecules. In order to plan and to carry out such an experiment, the scientist must have a store of theoretical knowledge, gained in decades of study. This means that a substantial amount of theory precedes the performance of the experiment.

As early as the eighteenth century, when scientists were not yet capable of carrying out such sophisticated experiments, Hume discovered that it is impossible to infer a scientific theory from experimental findings. We cannot use logical operations to infer theoretical conclusions from the experimental data. We explained that Russell considered Hume's conclusion intolerable in the sense that it undermined the rational basis of science.

For Kant this was a serious challenge: How is science possible? Kant's answer is hard to understand, but revolutionary: "[Human] *understanding does not derive its laws* from [nature], *but prescribes them to nature*" (*Prolegomena to Any Future Metaphysics*, Section 36). We obtain the basic laws of nature a priori. We have within us a supreme law of nature, in our intelligence and wisdom, and we must search for these laws there. According to Kant, a human being is capable of discovering synthetic a priori assumptions (new knowledge) that constitute a basis for the fundamental laws. How is this possible? This is the character of human intelligence.

How can we discover the laws of nature, when it is impossible to infer these laws from experience? Popper had claimed that he solved this problem. His solution is simple. Popper agrees with Kant that scientific theories are built *a priori*. What a scientist proposes as a theory is, in actuality, an a priori claim, and not a logical conclusion from the findings of the experiment. However, according to Popper, theories are only hypotheses, guesses. We can investigate whether these hypotheses do not contradict the findings of the experiment. We can corroborate them through a series of experiments that confirm them *prima facie*, but we cannot verify the theory or prove that it is true (unless we carry out an infinite number of experiments, including future ones).

Is it possible to prefer one hypothesis to another? We cannot verify a hypothesis, but we can refute it. To do so, it is sufficient that we conduct even one experiment that contradicts or disproves the theory. A hypothesis that has not yet been disproved is preferable to one that has been disproved already. If we wish to compare two theories of gravity, that of Einstein to that of Newton, we should say that Einstein's theory is preferable, since Newton's theory was disproved, and Einstein's has not been disproved (yet).

Both Kant and Popper agree that men create scientific theory. The difference between them is that Kant asserts that a priori knowledge is absolute, while Popper assumes that a theory is only a *hypothesis*.

However, the difference between Kant and Popper is not as great as it seems. In Einstein's opinion: "[T]he development of physics has shown that at any given moment, out of all conceivable constructions, a single one has always proved itself decidedly superior to all the rest. Nobody who has really gone deeply into the matter will deny that in practice the world of phenomena uniquely determines the theoretical system, in spite of the fact that there is no logical bridge between phenomena and their theoretical principles..." (*Ideas and Opinions*, 222). In other words, at times a brilliant scientist appears on the scene and succeeds, in an incomprehensible way, in arriving at the only theory that fits the experience, and "it has often been remarked how extraordinary this precision actually is" (Penrose, 556). Below we will return to the difference between the approaches of Kant and Popper (i.e., whether the new scientific theory is unambiguous).

We have seen how great philosophers such as Hume, Kant, Popper, and Einstein have dealt with the topic of scientific cognition. In any case, the question "how is science possible?" still stands. If it is impossible to infer laws of nature from experience, as Hume proved, then men themselves, their reason and intelligence are responsible for creating theory. Human intelligence is what discovers a priori (before the experiment) synthetic assumptions (new knowledge or new information). Still, there is no satisfactory answer to the question: "How can man obtain new knowledge, or be responsible for a new creation, *ex nihilo*?" Moreover, both Popper and Einstein admit that the creation of a new theory is a miracle.

We have arrived at a dead end. It stems from the anthropocentric approach, which places man at the center of a "man-centered universe." If man is not capable of logically inferring laws of nature from experimental findings, then he can extract laws of nature from his own intelligence a priori, before the experiment. However, a philosophic approach, which ignores divinity, does not answer the question of how man can determine laws of nature a priori. It arrives at a cul-de-sac, concluding that this is "a miracle" (in a secular framework!). This is the price that philosophy pays for ignoring God, and placing man in God's shoes.

This anthropocentrism is a general tendency that characterizes Kant's philosophy. He developed a system of autonomous morality, in which man is the unique source that determines what is good and what is bad. This is called the humanistic approach. In the opinion of Emil Fackenheim, a contemporary Jewish philosopher, it is a self-destructive approach.

Man's ability to divine laws of nature is a fact. Maimon concludes there is only one possibility of explaining this fact from a philosophical point of view. For this purpose, Maimon suggests the metaphysical idea of the infinite intelligence, and that man, using his intelligence, has a connection to this infinite intelligence. Now it is possible to understand in principle how man can produce synthetic a priori assumptions, i.e., new knowledge, or new information. All the knowledge of the world is at the disposal of the infinite intelligence, and the new knowledge, a synthetic a priori assumption that man extracts seemingly from his own intelligence, is no more than a part of the general knowledge characterizing the infinite intelligence.

In this way, Maimon saves *rationalism*, the reasonability of the synthetic a priori assumption. Without Maimon's metaphysical hypothesis, the possibility of arriving at a synthetic a priori assumption seems unreasonable, almost mystical, and Popper would have to admit that the scientist's activity is mystical: "It is his intuition, his mystical insight into the nature of things, rather than his reasoning, which makes a great scientist…. *Creativeness is an entirely irrational, mystical faculty…*" (*The Open Society and Its Enemies*, 2:228; emphasis mine).

Indeed, Maimon's approach is considered innovative in the realm of general philosophy. However, from a Jewish philosophical point of view, there is no impressive innovation here—we clearly detect the influence of Maimonides.

Above we noted (section 2.5) that a new physics theory, such as Einstein's general theory of relativity, is a new creation, *ex nihilo*. Before Einstein formulated his general theory of relativity, this theory did not exist. Maimonides emphasizes (2.7) that man's ability for intellectual achievement, to create as it were *ex nihilo*, exists "*because of the divine intellect conjoined with man.*" We can arrive at a rational explanation of man's ability to make synthetic a priori assumptions and to create new knowledge *ex nihilo*, when we take into account the connection of the human intellect to the divine intellect: "intellect which overflowed from Him…toward us is the bond between us and Him" (*Guide of the Perplexed* 3:51). R. Soloveitchik formulated this beautifully: "God created the world as a separate and discrete entity, but did not grant it independent reality. The world exists because it suckles from the infinite being of God" ("*U-bikashtem mi-sham*," 202–203).

The bottom line is that science, scientific knowledge, and the basic laws of nature are all the revelations of God. Clearly, man cannot know in advance how to predict when a certain revelation will take place. This is part of the divine plan, God's wisdom. The revelation on Mount Sinai and the giving of the Torah were part of the divine plan; the revelation of the laws of nature is a continuation of the implementation of this plan. In the history of science, first came the mathematics of the Greeks. This was followed by classical physics, Einstein's relativity theory, and quantum physics; each of these was accompanied by further developments in mathematics.

We might ask the following: how can we resolve divine revelation with Popper's philosophy that each new phase in science disproves or falsifies the previous stage? For example, Einstein's theory negates Newton's theory. If this is so, how is it possible that God reveals to man an incorrect theory? In order to answer this question, we will recall the "correspondence principle" (Niels Bohr) which views the new theory as encompassing the old one within it, and the old theory as a specific case of the new. Therefore, Einstein's theory of relativity includes Newton's theory as a specific case, as long as the speed of bodies (such as rockets) is much less than the speed of light (300,000 km/second). Therefore, Newton's formulae of mechanics are valid for the computation of bodies moving at "normal" speeds, as the velocity of light is very much greater than the speed of rockets. The great precision of Newton's mechanics obviates the need for using Einstein's theory for most calculations, even though we could use it. Only at speeds close to the speed of light, such as for the movement of elementary particles, is Einstein's theory necessary.

Below is a schematic picture of different levels of scientific knowledge, which gradually become accessible to humanity. Each new level represents a new theory with all its limitations; it encompasses the lower level of the previous theory. Thus, we assume that a future theory will also encompass both Einstein's theory and Newton's, just as Einstein's theory encompasses Newton's theory. By "encompass" I mean that a new theory includes the old one as a particular instance. A new theory relegates the old to a limited area of parameters: for example, low speeds compared to the speed of light.

As we explained, it is impossible to validate any theory logically. In order to do this, we must execute an infinite number of experiments, including future ones. On the one hand, more than three hundred years have passed since Newton's discovery of mechanics; since then

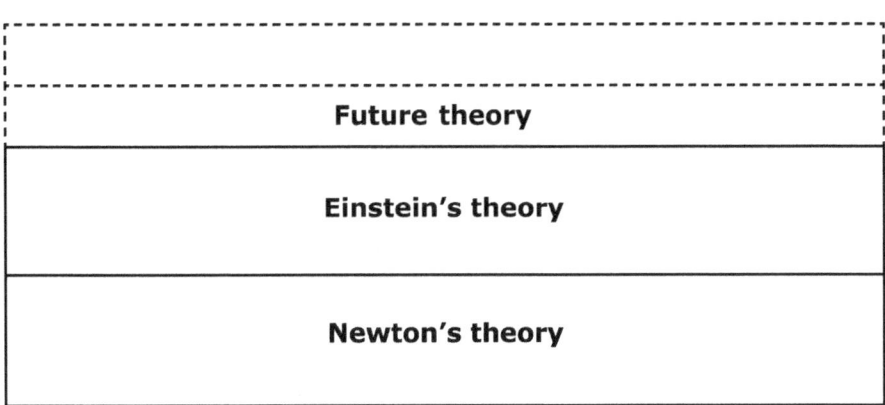

Accumulation of scientific knowledge over time

many experiments have been carried out, *and not one experiment has ever contradicted Newton's theory in its area of application.* Moreover, a new theory comes along—Einstein's—and it proves the truth of Newton's theory in the latter's field of application (assuming that Einstein's theory is true, or more exactly, that it is a better approximation of the truth). The new theory also determines the area of use of Newton's theory. In fact, Einstein's theory strengthened Newton's theory in its area of application, and determined its borders. They were not known before the formulation of Einstein's theory. Understandably, the new theory does not determine its own area of application. This can be done only by the future theory that will supplant the present one.

According to Popper's theory of scientific cognition, the discovery of Einstein's theory *refutes* Newtonian mechanics: Newton's theory is not valid for a certain area of parameters, for which Einstein's theory has not yet been disproved. This is the reason for preferring Einstein's theory. But we can look at the overall picture from another perspective. If until the appearance of Einstein's theory we had only experimental corroboration of Newton's theory, we now also have theoretical corroboration. Einstein's theory proves the truth of Newton's mechanics in its field of application. Einstein's theory leads to predictions and results that are almost identical with the predictions and conclusions of Newton's mechanics in its field of application, when the difference between them is so miniscule that we can ignore it for all practical purposes. Newton's mechanics stems theoretically from Einstein's theory, as a particular case, at speeds much lower than the speed of light.

A new theory not only determines the experimental field of implementation, but it opens new scientific vistas. The world of general relativity has nothing in common with a physical representation of the theory of Newtonian gravity, just as quantum theory opens a totally new world in physics. From this point of view, too, a new theory disproves an old theory and provides a better approximation of the truth.

We will now return to our principal conclusion: scientific knowledge and the fundamental laws of nature are divine revelations. We know that not everything that seems like a revelation is indeed so. There have been false prophets. However, the examination of the truth of a scientific revelation is quite solid. As we have noted, countless experiments have strengthened and confirmed the validity of Newton's mechanics in its field of application. The new level in our scientific knowledge (Einstein's theory) strengthened Newton's mechanics theoretically, and determined the borders of its applicability. The revelations of the new theory have offered a more solid foundation for Newton's mechanics than that previously known.

Here we see no contradiction with Popper's concept: when we have two hypotheses on the scales, the theory of Einstein is preferable. There are no experiments (yet) that contradict Einstein's theory, and on the other hand, there are experiments (new ones) that do not fit Newton's mechanics. The new information disproves Newton's mechanics in the field of high velocities. Yet at the same time, the new theory grounds Newton's mechanics for a limited field of parameters. In the same way, we can presume that a future theory will limit Einstein's theory but will ground it in the limited sphere of parameters. Thus new discoveries will add more and more layers of new knowledge, *ad infinitum*. Scientists, like Torah scholars, "do not rest either in this world or in the world to come." They "will go from strength to strength; each one will appear before God in Zion" (Psalms 84:8).

We might ask, in what way does the scientist arrive at an invention of something new? We will ignore here the question of whether all inventions are divine revelations. Nonetheless, it is possible to say with caution that each revelation is an invention. Why do I emphasize the word "invention"? What is the difference between a discovery and an invention? Columbus discovered America—it existed before he discovered it. Franklin invented the lightning rod—previously no such instrument existed.

Fifty years ago the renowned mathematician Jacques Hadamard set out to understand how mathematicians invent new ideas. In *The Psychology of Invention in the Mathematical Field*, Hadamard published a number of testimonies about inventions in the sphere of mathematics. We noted above (2.3) that mathematics is not very different from physics—in both areas we are unable to derive the laws through logical operations alone. Carl Friedrich Gauss related how he derived a certain mathematical law that he spent several years trying to prove: "Finally, two days ago, I succeeded, not on account of my painful efforts, but by the grace of God. Like a sudden flash of lightning, the riddle happened to be solved. I myself cannot say what was the conducting thread that connected what I previously knew with what made my success possible" (Hadamard, 15). The inventor Charles Nicolle said: "It is like a creation. Contrary to progressive acquirements, such an act owes nothing to logic or reason. The act of discovery is an accident" (ibid., 19).

The common ground in these testimonies, and many others, is that there are two types of processes that bring about an invention or a scientific achievement:

1. A process of logical operations, of rational thought. This process can be carried out by well-defined logical units of action such as algorithms (1.3). We can contemplate this process as though our personal computer, our brain, has performed it.

2. The second process has no connection to systematic logical thought. It is like a lightning flash in a very dark night sky. In contrast to the thought process, which is logical and consistent, a person does not control this second type of process. The "flash of lightning" comes to him; it is something that happens to him. It does not happen to every person. We must be ready for it, to be a worthy recipient. In days of old, there were schools for prophets. A person with no scientific training is not capable of academic achievement. Scientific training is a necessary condition but is not sufficient. The experience of a "flash" does not depend upon the person; he cannot summon it as a voluntary act.

Maimonides writes about processes of cognition that are similar in both divine and natural sciences:

> You should not think that these great *secrets* are fully and completely known to anyone among us. They are not. But sometimes truth flashes out to us so that we think it is day, and then matter and habit in their various forms conceal it so that we find ourselves again in an obscure night, almost as we were at first. We are like someone in a very dark night over whom lightning flashes time and time again.
> (*Guide of the Perplexed*, Preface, 7)

Generally speaking, we can say that *science is something that happened to humanity.* One of the signs of true revelation is that it changes reality. We cannot argue with the fact that the revelation on Mount Sinai changed life on earth—both spiritually and materially. Science is another revelation: it has caused, on another level, very significant changes in the life of mankind. We have already noted above (1.2) the population explosion that took place after the pace of scientific innovations increased markedly and began to influence human life.

I understand science as a religious act, but as a type of religious act different from what is generally accepted. Understanding science as a divine revelation is imperative in order to love God with all our hearts, with all our souls, and with all our might. Maimonides supports this position. Towards the end of his *Guide of the Perplexed* Maimonides presents the allegory of a king's palace within a city. As a person draws nearer to the palace and to the king, he also draws closer to God.

> Those who seek to reach the ruler's habitation and to enter it, but never see the ruler's habitation, are the multitude of the adherents of the Law, I refer to *the ignoramuses who observe the commandments.*
>
> Those who have come up to the habitation and walk around it are the jurists who believe true opinions on the basis of traditional authority and study the law concerning the practices of divine service, but do not engage in speculation concerning the fundamental principles of religion and make no inquiry whatever regarding the rectification of belief...
>
> Know, my son, that as long as you are engaged in studying the mathematical sciences and the art of logic, you are one of those who walk around the house searching for its gate, as the Sages ... have said resorting to a parable: *Ben Zoma is still outside* [Tractate Hagigah 15a]. If, however, you have understood the natural things, you have entered the habitation and are walking in the antechambers. If, however, you have achieved perfection in the natural things and have understood divine science, you have entered into the ruler's place *into the inner court* and are with him in one habitation. This is the rank of the men of science; they, however, are of different grades of perfection.
>
> There are those who set their thought to work after having attained perfection in the divine science, turn wholly toward God... These people are those who are present in the ruler's council. This is the rank of the prophets. (*Guide of the Perplexed* 3:51)

Understanding the structure—the metaphysics—of science, is one of the steps in reaching the level of prophecy. When we say that science constitutes a type of religious activity, we do not mean that mere occupation with science is what brings us closer to God. Rather, what will lead to proximity to God is occupying ourselves with understanding the world, and understanding the revelation of God as the source of science. Maimonides emphasizes explicitly that occupying oneself only with Torah is not sufficient to draw closer to God; occupying oneself with science in a broad sense is vital. He wrote this more than eight hundred years ago, and faced the opposition of many. Today as well, certain sectors of society oppose any contact with science, since in their opinion, it weakens and destroys faith.

Today, we are witnesses to God's revelation—science. Occupying ourselves with science and understanding its structure is vital for proximity to God. Ignoring and distancing ourselves from science only compounds ignorance, and alienates us from true faith. The Psalmist sang about this ignorance: "How great are Your deeds, O God, Your thoughts are very profound. A boor cannot know, nor can a fool understand this" (Psalms 92).

10. Second Conclusion: Science and Faith

Sometimes we place science and faith on opposite sides—"blind faith" in contrast to solid science. Let us think about the term "faith." Some argue that faith is relative, unverifiable, and without basis. I will now show that this assessment is imprecise.

I will start from the example that we discussed in the first chapter—free will. We cannot prove, either experimentally or through study, that a person has or does not have free will. However, I firmly believe that I have free will. This is also the basis for my faith in Judaism. As we have already noted, without free will, the commandments of the Torah have no meaning. Nevertheless, I have some highly educated and erudite colleagues who doubt the existence of free will. A short time ago, I heard a lecture by an expert on the brain. He ended with the sentence, "We must search for a biophysical mechanism of the illusion of human free will."

Here is another example. I believe in the existence of an external world (outside of myself). Most people are not conscious of this. They accept it as self-evident, even though it is, in fact, a belief whose truth cannot be proven.

These two examples of beliefs show that they are absolute from the point of view of the person holding them. My faith in freedom of choice needs no proof. It is something in my "self" that I feel, immediately and directly. I am using these examples as an introduction to a loftier belief, the belief in God, although the beliefs in the above examples are themselves part of belief in God. Many have attempted to prove God's existence, both in medieval and modern philosophy. After our analysis of the principle of induction, clearly we cannot point to any proof of the infinite based on finite reality. This is, in fact, the attempt to prove from the particular to the general. Thus, R. Soloveitchik wrote:

> We do not have permission to use categories born of a finite, dependent and temporary reality in order to prove the truth of an un-final, absolute and eternal reality. These categories, which are instrumental when used to determine formal-quantitative laws and to create a scientific plan of the world, cannot leave the circle of scientific experiment and rule without limits over a world that transcends the tangible, experiment, and reason. ("*U-bikashtem mi-sham,*" 127–28)

Just as I do not need to prove freedom of choice and the existence of the world (and there are no such proofs), neither do I need a formal proof of God's existence. There are those sublime (and rare) moments when I identify with what R. Soloveitchik wrote about those who feel God's presence directly. "Eternity can be felt directly and experienced immediately, like the tangible" (ibid., 129, footnote).

Belief in freedom of choice and belief in the external world are part of our faith in a divine reality. Again, I turn to R. Soloveitchik (ibid., 128–29):

> Awareness of reality in general, and of your own entity in particular, do not involve logical decisions; rather they are the spiritual essence

of a human, and it is similarly so vis-à-vis the experiencing of God. God is the source, the beginning and the end of the existence and reality of man. This does and will always precede all conclusions. It is absolutely certain, an absolute truth. If there is a world, and there is reality at all—and this no man who is not caught up in speculations can deny—then there is a Creator who is the Source of all life. As long as there is an "I," that is, as long as man exists (man is certain about this too), then there is a living, personal God that fills man with awareness of himself. It is impossible to think or even discuss the reality of the existence of the world if one does not live and feel the Source of life: "I shall be who I shall be."

The bottom line is that belief is certain and absolute and has no need for proofs. At any rate, it is not in the sphere of possible proof.

This is all well and good, but in any case, we might ask ourselves about the source of our faith. We have already determined the factuality of faith, which exists in different levels in each of us. The validity of our faith may not be provable, but the fact that we have, each of us, certain beliefs, is undeniable. However, we have not considered the question—from where does this faith come? The situation is very similar to the one Kant confronted when he asked about the source of science. Kant answered that the source of science is human reason. Our analysis has led us to the conclusion that the connection with the infinite intelligence is responsible for the new scientific knowledge that we accept as divine revelation. I think we can say something similar about faith. Clearly, faith is contained within the self of each one of us.

There is a parallel to this in new scientific knowledge, which exists within the self of the scientist who discovers it. However, the ultimate source both of scientific knowledge and of faith is God, to whom we are connected. In our prayers we say: "You graciously endow man with *knowledge*, and teach understanding to a frail mortal. Endow us graciously from Yourself with wisdom, understanding and *knowledge*. Blessed are You, gracious giver of *knowledge*." In the book of *Tanya* by

R. Shneur Zalman of Liadi, the word *knowledge* is interpreted as the attachment between man and God. A connection with God is the *objective* foundation of faith.

Now I return to the subject of science. In the first conclusion, I discussed the development of science, showing that a new theory encompasses the old, determining its limits and strengthening it in content. We called this the "correspondence principle." I said that science of this type is the revelation of God. Here I would like to emphasize a vital component of our conversation about the reciprocity between science and Judaism: there are no contradictions at all between basic science and Judaism, from Newton's mechanics to quantum theory. Mere statement of basic laws of nature does not contravene any of Judaism's principles.

However, the word "science" has several different connotations. There are scientific principles, and there are their applications. Usually one has to make additional assumptions, including metaphysical ones, on the way to achieve the applications. While there is no contradiction between Judaism and science's basic premises, a certain science application, may, in principle, be incompatible with Judaism, due to tacit usage of certain metaphysical assumptions. The Big Bang Theory, for example, describes the creation of the world as a unique event and therefore it is not a typical example of the application of science. Theories like this make additional assumptions and long-range extrapolations, which cannot be validated. This specific theory is also based on the metaphysical assumption that creation and development of the universe can be described by physics alone. I do not mean to say by this that the Big Bang Theory contradicts Judaism. However, it can hardly be considered to prove Judaism (as some try to do). I have already quoted R. Soloveitchik explaining that "we do not have permission to use categories born of a finite, dependent and temporary reality in order to prove the truth of an un-final, absolute and eternal reality."

Furthermore, the word "science" is also sometimes used to describe endeavors that have no connection whatsoever with basic scientific principles. An example is the use of the word "science" in the field of biblical criticism. Among its many assumptions, one is fundamental: the disregard for the connection between man and God, a connection that the very text under study often documents. A further example: witnesses to the Holocaust are still alive today, and yet there are so-called historians who assert that they have "scientific proof" that denies the Holocaust took place.

Contradictions between Torah and Judaism often appear in the context of this kind of "science." Perhaps this type of science is worthy of further analysis, but I will content myself with the observations already made.

Chapter Three

Evolution of Life

1. Introduction: Two Worldviews—Divine Providence, and a World without God

During the last few centuries, and especially in the nineteenth century and the first half of the twentieth, philosophers and intellectuals have tried to explain the world without God.

One of these was Karl Marx, who "explained" historical developments in economic terms. Marxism had such a strong influence on the world that entire parties and states identified with this theory. Empires arose, sacrificing millions of individuals on the altar of Marxism. For a long time, many of the Western intelligentsia identified with Marxism. Today, it is clear that both the theory and the attempt at implementation are a total failure.

Sigmund Freud "explained" the soul as a by-product of sexual motives. Freud's theory is still influential in some sectors today.

Both Marx and Freud were openly anti-religious, and their theories contributed to an anti-religious atmosphere in the intellectual world. In contrast, Charles Darwin, the nineteenth-century biologist, defined himself as a believing man and sometimes as an agnostic. Ironically, it was his theory of evolution, or "natural selection," which strengthened the anti-religious worldview more than any other contemporary scientific theory. At first glance, his theory (or later versions of it) seems to indicate the possibility of explaining the development of the world without God. According to the theory of evolution, we can explain the development of life on earth as a result of natural factors, both necessary and accidental.

In the eyes of many, the theory of evolution, which the following chapters will deal with, seems to contradict the worldview of the believer, especially that of the believing Jew. Therefore, we must emphasize the difference between facts and assumptions underlying the theory of evolution, and the worldviews that various philosophers and scientists have developed from those same facts and assumptions. Karl Marx and Friedrich Engels, the enthusiastic materialists of the nineteenth century, immediately recognized the implications of Darwin's achievements. In 1869, after the publication of Darwin's *The Origin of Species*, Marx wrote the following to Engels: "Although he [Darwin] writes and expresses himself in a rough English style, this book upholds the basis of the natural history that parallels our views."

Today, many still use Darwinism (or neo-Darwinism, in its modern form) for justifying the materialist and atheist approach. This approach sees the development of the world in general, and specifically the development of life on earth, as an expression of the activity of the forces of *materia*, matter, without the intervention of any external cause. Matter and its movements are sufficient to explain all phenomena in the world, including life, self-awareness, the soul, and human emotion.

In contrast, the concept of divine providence lies at the foundation of Judaism's entire perspective. According to the Jewish viewpoint, God rules the world; He directs and determines everything that takes place within it. Judaism attributes great importance to the concept of general and personal providence. The first of the Ten Commandments is, "I am the Lord your God who brought you out of the Land of Egypt, out of the house of bondage." In this commandment, God conveys to us the fundamental truth of

His role in history. Maimonides counts faith in divine providence as one of the thirteen basic principles that each Jew is required to believe: "I believe with complete faith that the Creator, may His Name be blessed, knows all the deeds of human beings and their thoughts, as it is said, 'He fashions their hearts all together, He comprehends all their deeds.'"

However, divine providence applies not only to human beings, but to all the creatures on earth. The first sentence of the Torah teaches us to understand God as the Ruler of nature. The Babylonian Talmud tells us, "God sits and sustains life, from a buffalo's horns to nits" (Tractate Shabbat 107b). The kabbalah combines the idea of divine providence with the assumption that there is a system, characterized by organization and continuity, for directing the world. Divine forces, known in kabbalah as *sefirot*, rule this system, and they are revealed through their direction of the world. R. Soloveitchik describes this process precisely: "God created the world as a separate and distinct entity, but did not grant it independent reality. *The world exists because it suckles from the infinite Being of God*" ("U-bikashtem mi-sham," 202; emphasis mine).

We have before us two worldviews. One is the theocentric—God is the center of the world; He runs it and intervenes in what takes place in it. The development of the world, including the animal kingdom, is under divine supervision or providence. The other worldview is the atheist-materialist or secular one. This viewpoint sees us, our inner world, the abundance of life forms, human society, economics, beliefs, feelings of love, hate, and jealousy as products of only one single cause: *materia* and its movement. These two outlooks constitute metaphysical positions, and as such, they are not derived from experience or from theory. Thus we can see the materialistic position as a form of faith. We have already seen in chapter 1 that the materialistic belief is unreasonable and irrational.

Many have derived far-reaching conclusions from Darwinism, as if the "theory of evolution" leads to the materialistic worldview. They conclude that there is a conflict between this theory (along with neo-

Darwinism) and the Jewish faith. This imagined contradiction is what deters many in certain religious circles from any contact with Darwin's theory of evolution (Israel's national-religious school curriculum does not include this theory at all). This restraint is unjustified. I will endeavor to demonstrate this in the following discussion of neo-Darwinism.

I set two goals for myself. One of them, quite modest, is to show that the theory of evolution, in its standard and accepted form, is compatible with the concept of divine providence, and does not contradict it. There is compatibility between the evolution of life, as described in the theory of evolution, and the belief in divine providence. My second goal is to provide a general analysis of the foundations and assumptions of the theory of evolution. The findings of this analysis undermine the basis of any theory of evolution.

2. *The Basic Mechanism of Natural Selection*

The theory of evolution rests on the following basic premises:

1. The profusion of life-forms on earth originates from several organisms, or even from only one; we speak of an evolutionary "tree," an evolutionary history.
2. The theory of evolution that explains this process includes the following hypotheses:
a. *Heredity*: Offspring reconstruct their parents' hereditary material, and thus they reconstruct their parents' organism with great fidelity. Heredity is, in general, a stabilizing factor that tends to preserve a common pattern for individuals in subsequent generations. The oak tree that grows from the acorn is similar to the tree that produced the acorn. A chick that hatches from an egg is similar to the hen that laid it. However, we know that offspring are not a precise copy of their parents. Evolution (no

matter in which direction) is a process of change, in which the differences between the offspring and their parents are of utmost importance.

b. *Change*: There are three possible reasons for change.
   i. First of all, the development of the individual is influenced not only by heredity, but also by the *environment*. Two oak trees, even if they sprout from two identical acorns, do not have the same form, size, or number of leaves. Differences in the environment, such as soil type and weather, influence the trees' growth. The environment in general influences plants more than animals. Among types of animals, mammals are the least influenced by the environmental factor. Environmental changes are not hereditary; they are not preserved in the subsequent generations.
   ii. According to the theory of evolution, an additional factor leads to differences between offspring and their parents: the *mechanism of sexual reproduction*. This mechanism is nearly (but not completely) universal both among plants and among animals. The offspring receive different genes from two parents. The parents transfer a combination of genes to their offspring, a set identical neither to the father's set of genes nor to the mother's. This mechanism brings about an infinite number of hereditary variations within the same family, but does not cause the creation of a new type or species.
   iii. The main factor capable of making a long-term evolutionary change is *mutation*: a random change in the hereditary material. There are different causes for the appearance of mutations, amongst them radiation.

c. *Natural Selection*: According to the theory of natural selection, evolution, or the development of life, is neither totally random nor totally directed, but constitutes a combination of these two types of processes. Mutations are accidental, but adaptation to the environment is deliberate. The idea behind natural selection is rather simple, although its operation is most complex and delicate. In every population, some individuals have more offspring than others. Individuals whose hereditary changes are more positive will survive, while individuals with unsuccessful hereditary characteristics will die before giving birth to a continuing generation. Changes that are passed down result in phenomena of *differential* survival, which accumulate from generation to generation. In this way natural selection acts to constantly improve and preserve the adaptations of life-forms and plants to their environment and way of life.

The basic mechanism under the rubric "natural selection" includes three components: heredity, mutation, and natural selection. Since Darwin, biology has made great advances, and today we are well informed about the physics and chemistry of the mechanism of heredity. We are capable of deciphering man's genetic code, but the mechanism of natural selection is still considered the basis for understanding evolutionary change.

The mechanism of natural selection is a vital tool for understanding biological phenomena. For example, we can explain the adaptation of bacteria to certain antibiotics such as penicillin through the mechanism of natural selection. Another example is *protective mimicry*, where animals such as birds and insects develop a resemblance to the colors and patterns of their natural surroundings as a means of hiding from their predators. We have no alternative to natural selection for describing, explaining, and understanding these and many other biological phenomena.

3. *The Molecular Basis of Life Processes*

(*The reader may skip this section if desired, as it is not necessary for understanding the general argument.*)

Over the last fifty years, the molecular mechanism of life has been gradually understood and deciphered. Below we will offer a schematic description of this mechanism.

The hereditary information of a living organism is present in its genes, which are composed of DNA molecules. These DNA molecules are made up of "code words," different combinations of the four "building blocks." The RNA molecules use this information in the DNA in order to build different proteins, which construct cells with various functions. This principle is known as the "central dogma" of biochemistry.

The code words in the RNA are taken from the molecules of the DNA. All our hereditary characteristics are stored in the DNA. In contrast, most of the RNA molecules hold information about only one of the many cell components. In general, one RNA molecule holds information about one gene.

Among the molecules within the cells, three types have special importance: proteins, RNA, and DNA. All of these are macromolecules made of polymers, which are built from secondary units called monomers.

A. Proteins

The proteins are the main materials responsible for the processes of life. The cell molecules that interact are, generally, quite stable. Without outside intervention, reactions between cell molecules are very slow. The role of the proteins is to expedite the biological reactions and to bring them to speeds necessary for the processes of life. Protein is an *enzyme* that accelerates its own specific reaction. This selectivity is a specific characteristic of the enzyme, or biological catalyst. Proteins are macromolecules built out of polymerization of secondary units, the amino acids. (Polymerization is a chemical reaction in which small molecules combine to form larger molecules.) The enzymes' action is dependent on their spatial structure, which is dictated by their chemical structure, a sequence of the amino acids. The following diagram shows the general structure of the polypeptide chain, which is a result of polymerization:

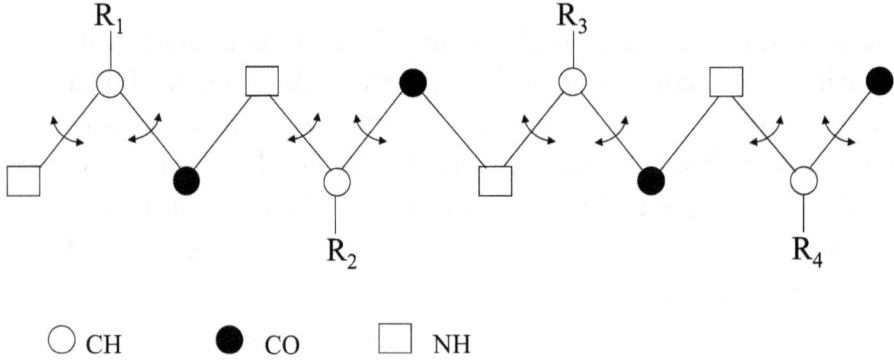

○ CH   ● CO   □ NH

R1, R2, R3, etc., represent the twenty amino acids that are the universal components of proteins. Below are several examples of amino acids:

Phenylalanyl (PHE)

Tyrosyl (TYR)

Tryptophanyl (TRY)

Prolyl (PRO)

Cysteinyl (CYS)

Methionyl (MET)

The polypeptide chain, built of amino acids, is folded up in a complex form around the globular, three-dimensional protein. Among the various forms that a protein might theoretically take, only one form actually materializes. This form determines certain protein-enzyme characteristics, both enzymatic and cognitive (how they recognize their specific reactions). The linear order of the amino acids in the polypeptides determines the protein's structure and characteristics.

The nucleic acids (DNA and RNA) are macromolecules built by polymerization of compounds called nucleotides.

B. DNA, the genetic code

The order of the amino acids of the polypeptide-protein is determined according to the order of the nucleotides in that section of the DNA chain. Accordingly, the order of the nucleotides in the DNA chain is the genetic code, which supplies the information about the composition of all the proteins in the organism's cells.

DNA (deoxyribonucleic acid) is composed of sequences of four nucleotides that are differentiated by their base formats, containing nitrogen. These four bases are known by their letter symbols: adenine—A, guanine—G, cytosine—C, and thymine—T. The specific order of the nucleotide bases in the DNA chain determines the structure of the proteins, which makes A, G, C, and T the letters of the genetic alphabet. DNA is made of two polynucleotide chains. In the double chain, A of one chain is always connected to T of another chain; G always connects to C; T to A; and C to G. Therefore, the order of the nucleotides in one chain determines the order in another chain. As there are twenty amino acids in proteins and only four "letters" (four nucleotides) in the genetic alphabet, several nucleotides are necessary in order to determine each amino acid. In fact, the code operates in threes: the order of three nucleotides determines each amino acid. For example, the amino acid aspartyl is determined by the nucleotides T, G, and A, in the order GAT; the amino acid glycyl is determined by the nucleotides A, G, and G, in the order GGA.

The genome (the genetic code) of a complex organism is very large. Even the DNA content of a relatively simple bacteria cell is large. The genome of the virus SV40 in monkeys includes 5243 basic pairs, in five genes. Genes of mammal cells contain around 2,500 million pairs of DNA nucleotides. The rows of the nucleotides are arranged in discrete sections of information or individual genes. The genome of the mammal contains around 50,000 to 100,000 genes. Each gene is responsible for the structure of what the gene produces—in general, a protein.

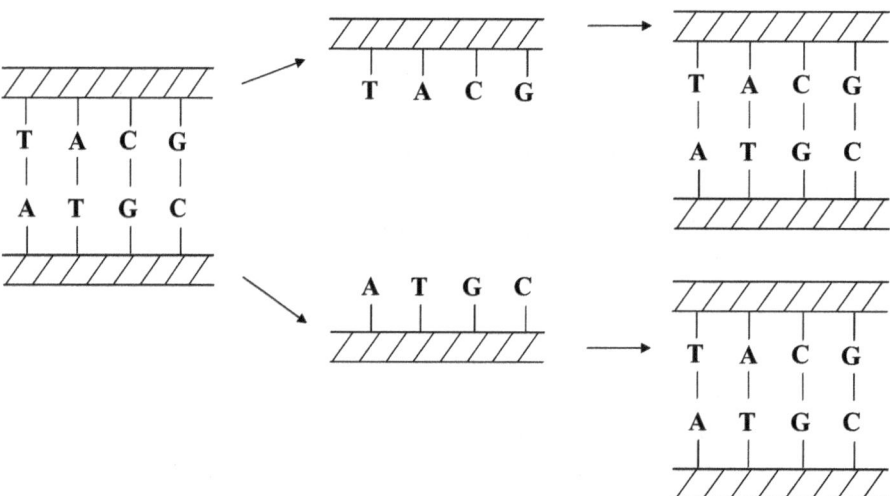

The *replication* of the double chain of the DNA (the double helix), takes place by the separation of the double chain into two strands, and the reformation of two duplexes from each separate part. The separated chain, the polynucleotide, attracts T to its A; A to T; C to G; G to C. The above picture shows the process of doubling for four pairs.

The two molecules that are created in this way are identical to the original molecule. However, mutations can disrupt this microscopic mechanism, creating new molecules that are different from the original.

C. RNA, the translation of the genetic code

The translation does not take place in the DNA chain itself, but in the replication of sections from one of the DNA chains to the RNA (ribonucleic acid). The RNA polynucleotides differ from the DNA in the exchange of the nucleotide U (uracil) in place of T (thymine). The mechanism of translation is quite complex, as shown in the following diagram:

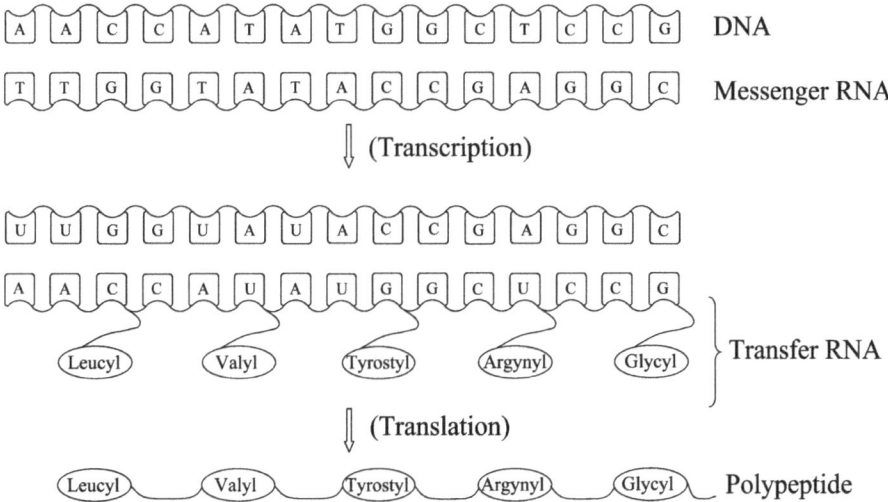

The RNA molecules serve as "mediators" between the DNA and the proteins. First the process of replication takes place; the "text" is written in a segment (one gene) of one of the DNA chains. This process takes place through the messenger RNA (mRN). The "message" from the messenger RNA is copied by the transfer RNA (tRNA), and passes to the ribosome. In fact, the transfer RNA is part of the ribosome. *The ribosome is the factory for the cells that translate the genetic code.* The ribosomes create proteins from the amino acids with great speed and precision according to the information in the genes, which the RNA brings after being copied from the DNA. Within the ribosome, special enzymes identify the amino acid and the specific transfer RNA, and catalyze the creation of a connection between the amino acid and the RNA molecules.

4. *DNA>>> RNA>>> Proteins>>> Cells>>> Organism*

(*This section includes a substitute for the previous segment, as well as its continuation and conclusion.*)

The heading of this section expresses the concept of so-called *central dogma.* The genetic information of the living organism is found within the DNA molecules. The RNA "reads" each section of the information encoded in the DNA, and uses this partial information for building the organism's cell proteins. Recently biologists, mathematicians, and theoreticians have developed a certain resistance to this central dogma, seeing it as too simplified to serve as a basis for theoretical calculations (K. Brown, "The Human Genome Business Today," *Scientific American,* July 2000, 40).

To generalize, we can say that living organisms, ranging from the simplest one-celled organisms to mammals to human beings, are highly complex and delicate mechanisms. What sets living things apart from inanimate objects is the hereditary material that is common to each living entity. From the simplest bacteria to plants and human beings, all have the same hereditary material—DNA—and humans are different only in the length of the DNA chain.

The hereditary material of the biological organism is largely preserved in subsequent generations, but we can identify miniscule changes from generation to generation as well as changes in various characteristics of the same species. Scientists estimate that 99.99% of human genes are identical, and the difference in hereditary material among individuals finds expression in just 0.01% of this hereditary material, the DNA.

The truly astonishing accomplishment in biology in the last hundred years has been the attainment of an understanding that every living organism contains uniform hereditary material that is the most conservative component of the organism (Darwin did not have this information). The hereditary material determines most of the physical characteristics of the living creature. A complete living organism develops from semen ("From whence do you come? From a stinking drop..." Ethics of the Fathers 3:1). The hereditary material includes all the necessary instructions for developing the organism from the semen. These instructions are written in "letters" and "words" that make up a certain language, like a computer language. Of course, this is only a simile: there is no real connection between the language of DNA and human language or computer language. But this comparison highlights the possibility that other languages exist beyond humanly created ones.

The hereditary material located in the DNA of the organism's cells includes an entire series of directions for developing the organism. For those who read the previous section (3.4), we described how the hereditary material in the DNA chain determines the structure of biomolecules vital for the functioning of the living organism, and for many kinds of proteins. A certain combination of different molecules determines a certain specific protein, and these molecules are like different "letters" of the hereditary "text."

Now suppose that we know nothing of genetic biology. We ask ourselves, how can the hereditary instructions be written up? The letters of such a text must be preserved over millions of years. The text itself changes gradually, because of mutations, but the letters of the text are preserved. All material that we are familiar with from daily experience can be eroded. Here we arrive at a crucial point. The letters of the hereditary text are made of molecules. These letters are not the products of human beings, but are "the finest masterpiece ever achieved along the lines of the Lord's quantum mechanics" (Schrödinger, *What Is Life?*).

In all living creatures and plants, hereditary information is stored in a uniform way, in the form of polynucleotides (a chain of molecules called nucleotides). In general, the size of these chains is in proportion to the size of the organism. Common viruses have between one thousand and one hundred thousand nucleotides, bacteria between a million and one hundred million, and vertebrates and plants more than one hundred million. The hereditary information in a human being is stored in around 10,000,000,000 nucleotides (since the nucleotides are arranged in pairs and the information stored in two chains, the length of one is 5,000,000,000 nucleotides).

If we write out the hereditary information of a human being in English letters, for example, we will fill more than two hundred telephone books. Together, these books will weigh about one ton, and their combined volume will be about one cubic meter. Yet the hereditary information of a human being is concentrated in the cell's nucleus, whose volume is 0.001 cubic millimeter! (However, we must take into account that not all the DNA is the source of hereditary information. There are many DNA molecules that do not have any hereditary function. It is not clear, yet, what is their significance; research into the matter is ongoing.)

This data offers only meager support for a mode of thinking free from prejudices about life in general and human beings in particular. Unfortunately, habit and routine prevent us from grasping the miracle of life. The hereditary information in man's cells adds nothing to our understanding of the phenomenon of the soul. We are used to being surrounded by creatures that are capable of both speaking on the one hand, and hearing and listening on the other; of feeling, and inspiring feelings of love, hate, empathy, jealousy, sympathy, and antipathy; of behaving rationally and irrationally. We are habituated to these things, like a child who is accustomed to television and cars and thus feels no sense of wonder at these modern inventions.

We can imagine (but only imagine!) an opposite situation (that cannot be realized). A physicist lives in another world devoid of life. He is an expert in quantum physics, the general and special theory of relativity, physical chemistry, and solid state physics—in short, he knows everything about inanimate material. His worldview is simple. Physics is capable of explaining all properties of matter. After all, everything in the world is matter (for the sake of this thought experiment we are ignoring the problem of the scientist's very existence). All the scientist's personal experience and observations support his worldview. He can explain everything in the world.

Then it so happens that the scientist moves to our planet, to earth. Here he experiences many miracles, and he views with wonder the profusion of animal and plant forms. In his eyes, the greatest marvels are the living creatures, especially human beings. Cars, television, and supercomputers do not amaze our scientist, for he easily explains them as the work of humans. However, the people—who talk, explain, argue, feel different emotions, react rationally and irrationally, and have freedom of choice—do not fit in with the scientist's previous worldview, i.e., that everything in the world is matter or made of matter. And everything obeys laws of physics only. His objective analysis leads him to conclude the existence of a being that creates everything, including the human beings themselves.

Before our scientist had arrived on earth, he did not think in this direction. He had believed that matter had always existed, and knew how to explain and understand all its qualities. However, from his conversations with his colleagues, the earthling scientists, he realized that they held a different opinion. They thought that the living world, including man, was created as a result of *evolution*, and that this evolution had a *creative* force. The scientists explained to him that they have a theory of evolution that aptly describes this process. Our scientist is not really convinced, and he begins to contemplate this matter. Without entering into the details of biology, he wants to understand if it is logically possible to derive the *theory* of evolution. Is a law of evolution possible at all? Now we shall leave our imaginary scientist alone, and endeavor to answer these questions by ourselves.

5. The Development of Life on Earth: Can We Prove the Theory of Evolution?

When we speak of evolution, we must distinguish between two different concepts. On the one hand, we speak of the *theory* of evolution: this is allegedly based on the mechanism of adaptation called natural selection (above, 3.2). On the other hand, we can also point to the *fact* of evolution, meaning the development of the profusion of life on earth, which began from primitive organisms and developed gradually into self-conscious creatures(that is, creatures who have consciousness of a self). Confusing these two ideas may lead to serious misunderstanding. We must also differentiate between the mechanism of adaptation, or natural selection, and the "theory of evolution." Sometimes scientists consider a successful explanation of a certain phenomenon of adaptation by the mechanism of natural selection as proof of the "theory of evolution."

The *fact* of evolution is established based neither on one theory or another, but on paleontological data—on the fossilized findings of animals from different periods. Note that evolutionary scientists today dispute the idea of gradual evolution as a factor for creating new species. Niles Eldridge and Stephen J. Gould explained the lack (or at least the rarity) of intermediate fossil sequences by asserting that evolution is not gradual. They hypothesized that when new species develop, they do so over a relatively short period of thousands of years. Before and after the change, the species remains stable for long periods, running into millions of years. Scientists call this type of development *punctuated equilibrium*.

The main thesis of the analysis below is that we cannot derive the *theory* of evolution (which describes the process of evolution) from paleontological data, which only establishes the *fact* of evolution, assuming that it is, indeed, a fact.

I will briefly re-summarize the main tenets of Karl Popper's theory of scientific cognition (2.5). He showed that all scientific theories are deductive, and logically derived from certain basic assumptions, which are the products of human creation. We cannot derive them logically from observations and experiments. We can test a theory with experiments and corroborate it by applying it to additional experiments. We must be able to refute or falsify the theory. But, as we have said, we cannot verify any theory absolutely. If we cannot test a theory by experiment, then this theory is not scientific but metaphysical.

Now we will ask ourselves: Assuming that it exists, what is the status of the theory of evolution? Here is Karl Popper's answer. The evolution of life on earth is a unique historical process, one of a kind. "Such a process, we may assume, proceeds in accordance with all kinds of causal laws, for example, the laws of mechanics, of chemistry, of heredity and segregation, of natural selection, etc. Its description, however, is not a law, but only a singular historical statement" (*The Poverty of Historicism*, 108).

Clearly, any theory, no matter how it is formulated, must be tested by new experiments before it merits the status of a law of nature. We cannot discover any law of nature if we remain attached to a one-and-only experiment.

This general philosophical understanding, based on logic, leads us to the unequivocal conclusion that the theory or law of evolution does not exist (or more exactly cannot be based upon known data).

Several biologists have also come to this conclusion in light of their research findings. In 1965 Jacques Monod, Andre Lwoff, and Francois Jacob won the Nobel Prize for their contribution to the field of genetic biology. Monod writes, "The thesis that I shall present in this book is that the biosphere does not contain a predictable class of objects or of events but constitutes a particular occurrence, compatible indeed with first principles, but not *deducible* from those principles and therefore essentially unpredictable" (*Chance and Necessity*, 43). Moreover, he adds, "I believe that we can assert today that a universal theory, however completely successful in other domains, could never encompass the biosphere, its structure and its evolution as phenomena deducible from first principles" (ibid., 42).

If we were to tape the whole evolutionary process on film, every rerun would be a new film, showing a completely different history. With this vivid metaphor, Gould presents the idea that evolution is unpredictable. The key word is "contingency," meaning dependency, or the possibility of an event. "A historical explanation does not rest on direct deductions from laws of nature, but on an unpredictable sequence of antecedent states, where any major change in any step of the sequence would have altered the final result. This final result is therefore dependent, or contingent, upon everything that came before" (*Wonderful Life*, 283).

George Gaylord Simpson, in his book *The Meaning of Evolution*, uses other words like "opportunistic" and "pragmatic" in order to describe the interdependent chain of events that make up the evolutionary process.

Doubtless, the mechanism of natural selection fulfills an important role in understanding the evolution of life on earth. But it is a great leap from this point to claiming that natural selection explains the evolution of life on earth. Of course, this depends upon how we understand the word "explain." The prevalent opinion is that the mechanism of natural selection explains all evolution on earth, and that from the moment life began (I am purposely abstracting myself from the problem of *creation* of life on earth) we can predict the development of life on earth. However, we have seen that it is impossible to make this prediction.

We can sum up the analysis of this section in Popper's words:

> There exists no law of evolution, only the historical fact that plants and animals change, or more precisely, that they have changed. The idea of a law which determines the direction and the character of evolution is *a typical nineteenth-century mistake, arising out of the general tendency to ascribe to the 'Natural Law' the functions traditionally ascribed to God.* (*Conjectures and Refutations*, 340; emphasis mine)

6. Compatibility with Divine Providence

In 1995, the National Association of Biology Teachers (NABT) in the US included on their agenda a vote on the public statement that "evolution is an unsupervised, impersonal, unpredictable and natural process." After hours of argument, the members of the association agreed to remove the words "unsupervised" and "impersonal." The president of the NABT, W. W. Carley, who insisted on the change, said that this change was in the spirit of good and honest science and that the assumption that "evolution is unsupervised" is a theological assumption (E. J. Larson and L. Witham, "Scientists and Religion in America," *Scientific American*, September 1999, 81). In the end, the NABT summed up, "Evolution is an unpredictable and natural process." However, this is not the accepted opinion among all biologists. Many of them insist that evolution is indeed an unsupervised and impersonal process.

We do not know which side is in the majority, and this is unimportant, as the majority does not decide in this case. What is important is that we cannot decide which side is right since the decision is in the metaphysical realm, as we made clear in the previous section. The question of whether or not the evolutionary process is controlled by divine providence is a question of faith. What we may say is that divine providence is compatible with the accepted picture of the evolution of life on earth; faith in divine providence does not contradict the accepted picture of evolution. I have purposely used the inexact term "accepted picture" instead of "the theory of evolution," since the theory of evolution does not exist, as we have clarified above.

We cannot connect the explanation of evolution with predictability; there is no theory which allows evolutionary development to be predicted. However, we can also widen this explanation by including in it random factors such as mutations, which cannot be predicted. And many biologists believe that the evolution of life on earth can be explained by the mechanism of natural selection. Here we must immediately express a reservation, as this assumption enters the field of metaphysics, and it is impossible to prove this explanation by experiment. There is no proof (see above) that natural selection alone can explain the evolution of life on earth, even though this is the accepted explanation of many biologists. In other words, this explanation or "theory" is a matter of faith.

Let us return to the problem of compatibility with divine providence. Clearly, the concept of evolution activated by natural selection is compatible with divine providence. What human beings conceive of as a "random" factor (mutation) may be, in fact, a divine action, just as we may interpret a consistent message in an unfamiliar language as being totally random. We conclude that the standard explanation of evolution does not contradict the possibility of divine providence; in fact, it fits well.

Many consider that the theory of evolution threatens religious belief, because of the widespread opinion that every development on the face of the earth, from unicellular organisms to *homo sapiens*, is predictable and predetermined, and we can explain it naturally. However, the random factor of mutation defies prediction of the entire process of development, and offers the possibility of different routes of evolution. The various routes of evolution can be either totally random, or in the hands of divine providence. The decision as to which possibility is realized lies outside the realm of experiment, and therefore, it is metaphysical.

Above we demonstrated the absence of proof that natural selection alone is enough to activate evolution, as well as the impossibility of proving such a claim. Evolution is a specific historical record, which cannot serve as a basis for any theory. This is an epistemological claim, belonging to the theory of cognition. We cannot discover or find a theory of evolution. Another question is whether the law of evolution exists at all, even if we are incapable of discovering it. This is an essential, ontological problem, to which we shall devote the next section.

To summarize this section, we must note an apparent self-contradiction. In the previous section, we proved that the fact of evolution (if it exists) does not determine a theory of evolution. In this section we have shown that if we ignore the problem of proving the "law of evolution," if we accept the law of evolution as an existing fact (or as a kind of metaphysical concept), then this law can coexist with belief in divine providence.

7. Does a Law of Evolution Exist?

Even though we are not able to discover, establish, or prove the law of evolution based on a specific historical record, such a law might indeed exist. We cannot, in principle, prove that this type of law exists or does not exist without additional assumptions. However, if we make a certain metaphysical assumption (that cannot be verified by experiment), then we will be able to prove that the law of evolution does not exist. Our basic premise is that man has free will. Indeed, this assumption seems self-evident, but it is metaphysical in character, as it cannot be tested either experimentally or theoretically. Rather, man senses his free will immediately and directly, and needs no logical reasoning in order to prove it. Faith in free will is one of the foundational beliefs of man, akin to the belief in the existence of other human beings. Each person bases his actions upon the assumption of his free will; the same may be said about his belief in the outer world. Therefore, we can accept freedom of choice as a basic premise or axiom.

In fact, one of the foundations of Judaism is that every development, every instance of evolution in life, is subject to divine providence. This is Judaism's basic outlook, notwithstanding the assumption that the laws of nature (physics, chemistry, biology) are true, including the mechanism of natural selection. Judaism acknowledges a natural order, and the adherence of the material world to established laws, which function, however, in accordance (and together) with providential involvement. We have seen that this concept is compatible with the standard explanation of the evolution of life.

Now we will ascertain whether the materialist, naturalist, and atheist view of evolution (so intrinsically alien to Judaism that Hebrew has no words for these terms) can coexist with the assumption of freedom of choice. According to the materialist outlook, in the early stages of the development of the world, only matter existed. Spiritual entities, such as the soul, spirit, and mind, appeared at a more advanced stage of the development of the world. In a naturalist, atheist, godless world, new objects cannot appear *ex nihilo*. Every new thing stems from a previously existing one, and, ultimately, from matter. Therefore, the spirit is derived from matter, and operates according to natural law. The worldview which says that every new thing is derived from something previous to it is called reductionism.

We know of two types of natural law. One is determinist in that previous events determine subsequent events in a definite manner. The second type of law is non-determinist; this kind of law determines only the probability of new events. In this context, it does not matter which type of law we are discussing, or, to be more precise, which law the world follows, so long as this law does not allow for new creation *ex nihilo*. Therefore, according to the naturalistic outlook, even when evolution reached the stage where there was such a thing as the human soul, natural law was the only determinant of its development. On the other hand, we believe that our individual wills also play a substantial role in the development of things, at least on earth.

Obviously, the laws of physics and chemistry influence change—human desire is not the only factor causing change or development. However, if free will exists, then the laws of nature cannot be the *only* reasons for all change. Human desires, aspirations, and choices can be influenced by logic, or by religious and moral considerations. Reading a book can change a person's behavior. If we accept that free will exists (and as we have said, this is a metaphysical premise that can neither be proven nor disproven in absolute terms, as it falls outside the realm of scientific verification), then we cannot accept that the self is regulated by biological laws alone. We arrive at the conclusion that the existence of free will contradicts the naturalist aspect of the law of evolution.

Until now, we have discussed the world as conceived by certain philosophers, who begin by placing limitations on it. In the next section, I will present my view of the real world, which assumes the existence of creativity and new creation. In order to describe the development of the world, I will use the term "creative emerging evolution"

8. *Creative Emerging Evolution*

Many philosophers commit the philosophical "sin" of dictating their own categories and worldview of reality. Their worldview might fall under the rubric of materialism with its assertion that the entire world is derived from matter, or under the heading of idealism with its own assertions. Aside from these general views, we are habituated to a number of supposedly self-evident axioms, which become philosophical dogmas. In the boxed text we consider an example of such a philosophical dogma.

> **Action on distance**
>
> Albert Einstein, for one, was strongly opposed to preconceived philosophical opinions, but even he could not guard himself from this mistake. He wrote, "But on one supposition we should, in my opinion, absolutely hold fast: the real factual situation in system A is independent of what is done with system B, which is spatially separated from the former" (Albert Einstein, *Albert Einstein, Philosopher Scientist*, ed. P.A. Schilpp, 1949, 85). Clearly, if two systems are so far removed from each other that no signal connects them over a certain period of time, they cannot have any influence over each other. However, it turned out that the validity of quantum theory implies the possibility of immediate action on distance, and it was Einstein who had first revealed this in 1948 ("*Quanten Mechanik und Wirklichkeit,*" *Dialectica* 2 [1948]: 320). Since then scientists have observed many cases in which system B had an immediate effect on system A (at infinite speeds). (See J. S. Bell, *Speakable and Unspeakable in Quantum Mechanics.*)

This example of a philosophical dogma is irrelevant to our analysis, and we only mention it here in order to clarify our meaning. Below is a philosophical dogma that is relevant to our analysis, termed in Latin *ex nihilo nihil fit*, meaning *ex nihilo* creation does not exist, or "there is nothing new under the sun."

Evidently this dogma stems from our limited daily experience. Long-range extrapolations may very well lead to erroneous conclusions. In any case, we may not turn a conclusion that is the product of our limited experience in both time and space into a philosophical dogma. The measure of truth of this dogma is very important, as it touches upon the very heart of understanding evolution.

Philosophers such as Herbert Spencer, Pierre Teilhard de Chardin, and Friedrich Engels saw evolution as the realization of a plan woven into a fabric within the structure of the world. A widespread trend is to view the stages of fetal development as a prototype of the stages of evolution. By contrast, the researcher J. Monod writes:

> For them [the above-mentioned philosophers], evolution is not really a creation but uniquely the "revelation" of nature's unexpressed designs. Whence the tendency to see in embryonic development an emergence of the same kind as evolutionary emergence. According to the modern theory, the idea of "revelation" applies to epigenetic development [development of the fetus], but not of course to evolutionary emergence, which owing precisely to the fact that it arises from the essentially unforeseeable, is the creator of *absolute newness*. (*Chance and Necessity*, 116; emphasis mine)

Let us develop this idea. According to any modern scientific theory, development in the world, or to be precise, development of the world, takes place in stages, beginning with lifeless matter. The first creation was the creation of the world itself. I do not mean the story of Genesis, but the standard theory of the Big Bang—a theory in physics that describes a new creation, creation *ex nihilo* (of course, we can always question the truth of this theory). We will skip certain stages of the world's development: the creation of stars, planets, galaxies, and heavy elements (these stages also include new creations, but not as clearly as in the creation of the universe) and go straight to the creation of life, which doubtless constitutes an act of creation *ex nihilo*.

From this point on, many new things are created: souls, the human spirit, works of human creativity in fields such as science, mathematics, philosophy, and art. Each of these fields includes a countless number of new creations. A new symphony, for example, is an *ex nihilo* creation. This symphony did not exist before its creation, and is not derived from former musical works. If we identify *ex nihilo* as a one-time act (and because of this, it does not fall under the rubric of science), that is to say as a miracle, then miracles are multiplying every day. "We shall give thanks to You...for Your wonders and Your favors that take place in each time, in the evening, morning, and afternoon" (daily *Amida* prayer, the blessing of thanks).

This picture explicitly contradicts accepted philosophical methods and dogmas. In this situation, only a philosopher who is not bound by prejudiced assumptions is capable of analyzing the matter objectively. Karl Popper is neither a materialist nor an idealist (with regard to philosophical theory). He considers himself a realist. He does not deny *ex nihilo* based on prior philosophical assumptions. He recognizes the idea of emerging development, and that although it contradicts all accepted concepts, it reflects reality:

> Whether or not we look at the universe as a physical machine, we should face the fact that it has produced life and creative men; that it is open to their creative thoughts, and has been physically changed by them.... [T]he universe that harbours life is creative in the best sense: creative in the sense in which the great poets, the great artists, the great musicians have been creative, as well as the great mathematicians, the great scientists, and the great inventors. (*The Open Universe*, 174)

In my opinion, Karl Popper had enough courage to look at reality as it is, even if this reality contradicts "common sense" and accepted philosophical dogmas such as the impossibility of an *ex nihilo* creation.

It is hard to say that philosophy has to follow in the footsteps of science. Indeed, the idea of creative evolution, or emerging development, has its source in a scientific approach. It does not contradict the latest scientific theories; on the contrary, it agrees with them. Nevertheless, it is not derived from them in a logical deduction, and it cannot be *reduced* to science. This point needs clarification. Possibly, science cannot explain creative emerging development, as every act of creation is one-of-a-kind. Science does not deal with unique events; they do not belong to the category we call science.

The relationship between science and creative emerging development has another aspect, connected to determinism or non-determinism. The determinist world (which is also reductionist, meaning each stage in development is derived from the previous one) acts with clockwork precision, with no deviations. It includes all organisms, animals, and people. From this view stems the negation of freedom of will, which is fundamentally incompatible with the determinist viewpoint.

Quantum theory has opened up a new option. We have learned that randomness and probability play an important role in the physical world, and this renders the scientific description of the world no longer determinist. Nonetheless, the situation is no clearer. To say that the black characters on the paper of a scientific article are random is no better than saying that these characters were derived at the time of the creation of the world. In both scenarios, creativity approaches zero. Is the combination of chance and necessity likely to improve the situation? For if evolution is activated by natural selection, such a combination is exactly what results.

We showed above that one cannot prove that natural selection is sufficient to initiate and explain evolution. This is a belief, and it has no basis in daily experience. We have never seen nor experienced new creation as a result of a combination of natural, necessary, and random factors. Likewise, no experiment has succeeded in creating a new biological species as a result of natural, necessary, and random factors. In the same way, we cannot predict a new biological species based on the "theory" of evolution.

Popper as a realist (but not as a materialist!) understood better and more clearly than his predecessors that the development of the world includes many incidents of true creativity, when something new is born that did not exist previously—*ex nihilo*. However, his description is phenomenological: he describes phenomena as they are, without entering into the essence of things, without asking (or answering) questions such as "why." The reason is that the essence is located outside of the intellectual, scientific approach. It is impossible to predict truly creative phenomena in a scientific manner; otherwise these phenomena would cease to be creative. If there were a theory of creativity, which enabled us to predict all possible scientific discoveries, then we would be able, as a matter of course, to discover all future scientific discoveries immediately. Creativity in scientific pursuit would then effectively disappear. And after all, each creative act is one of a kind, unique. Scientific research, by its nature, cannot be applied to the unique event.

Until now, we have acted with restraint and refrained from entering the field of religion. However, as we have arrived at a dead end in our intellectual, rationalistic path, we will try to let Jewish metaphysics assist us. After exhausting the arguments of physics, we turn to metaphysics. "God created man in His image, in the image of God He created him, male and female He created them" (Genesis 1:27). From this verse, we learn that some of man's characteristics make him similar to God. When we compare man to other animals, we identify creativity as the trait that most noticeably differentiates between them. If this is so, then we may conclude that man's creativity is one attribute that makes him similar to God. Thus, if we are looking for signs of divine activity in the development of the world, this activity must be creative. To use metaphorical language, the development of the world reveals signs of *personal* activity to us. These signs point to what we might call the *creativity of the universe*.

9. Conclusion: Evolution—Law of Nature or Divine Providence?

The basic mechanism called *natural selection* includes three components: heredity, mutation, and adaptation to the environment by natural selection. Mutations cause random changes in the hereditary material, and the hereditary mechanism passes them on to the following generations. The mechanism of natural selection can be explained as follows: in each population, some individuals will have more offspring than others. Individuals with more positive changes will, on average, survive, while those with less successful heredity will have fewer offspring. Therefore, natural selection acts continually to improve the adaptation of animals to their environment and to their way of life.

We must distinguish between the mechanism of adaptation by natural selection and the theory of evolution, just as we must distinguish between the *fact* of evolution and the *theory* of evolution. The "theory" of evolution presumes to explain the entire process of evolution of life on earth. Its basic assumption is that the mechanism of natural selection is responsible for the whole process of evolution. Ernst Mayr, Darwinism's enthusiastic supporter, wrote:

> Darwinism rejects all supernatural phenomena and causations. The theory of evolution by natural selection explains the adaptedness and diversity of the world solely materialistically. It no longer requires God as creator or designer (although one is certainly still free to believe in God if one accepts evolution). (Mayr, "Darwin's Influence on Modern Thought," *Scientific American* [July 2000]: 69)

Marx and Engels hastened to react to Darwin's *Origin of Species*. In their opinion, this work could have been the basis for a natural history that was compatible with their materialist worldview.

Many critics think that Darwinism, or, more precisely, neo-Darwinism, offers a meaningful challenge to the Jewish worldview, especially to faith in divine providence. The enormity of this challenge becomes clear if we note, in brief, the complexity of the biosphere, the system of life on earth. Man is the pinnacle of this complex system. If we write the hereditary text (DNA sequences) of man in ordinary letters, it will occupy about two hundred volumes of the *Hebrew Encyclopedia*. However, the hereditary text is written in molecules, and it occupies a volume of around 0.001 cubic milliliters. The hereditary text mainly determines the material or physical characteristics of man. However, man's complexity is determined first of all by his soul. We cannot imagine that such a sophisticated system can be created by a combination of random and necessary factors. Darwin spoke of "the extreme difficulty or rather impossibility of conceiving this immense and wonderful universe, including man with his capacity of looking far backwards and far into futurity, as a result of a blind chance or necessity" (E. Mayr, *One Long Argument*, 59).

On another occasion, Darwin writes, "The mind refuses to look at this universe, being what it is, without having been designed" (ibid.).

We must distinguish between the process of evolution, which is a type of historical record, and the theory of evolution. We proved (3.5) that we cannot establish a theory of evolution based on a unique record, just as we cannot determine a law based on one experiment. However, the impossibility of deriving a theory does not necessarily mean that the law does not exist. Here we enter the metaphysical area, as the existence or non-existence of this law cannot be tested by experiment (since we have only one "experiment," one historical or evolutionary record).

The premise of *freedom of will* is a metaphysical assumption, since we cannot test it through experimentation. This premise contradicts the existence of any *law* of evolution. We can imagine that evolution is directed by a certain law, but when it arrives at the stage of humanity, its development no longer follows this law, thus contradicting the basic truth of the law. The development of humanity is determined by the free choices of man together with the laws of nature. Freedom of choice is, in fact, the most basic faith without which human life, morality, and responsibility are meaningless. In the

Jewish view, the Torah and the commandments have meaning only when man has freedom of choice (1.2).

Until now, we have discussed the question of evolution. Can we derive the theory of evolution from paleontological data? If not, does this law still exist in principle? We concluded above that the law of evolution does not exist. Thus we can ask the following question: what causes evolution? We know of two kinds of developments. One is development directed by the laws of nature—we concluded that evolutionary development is not of this kind. We can explain the second kind of development using human life as an example. An individual life is directed not only by the laws of nature, but also by personal choices and decisions. The development of this individual is described as a biography.

The concept of evolution applies to every slow, gradual change of a personality or reality, both material and spiritual. We spoke of two kinds of development. Let us begin with the first. The laws of nature control the first type, and the system is the activating factor for its own development. We may use the Big Bang theory of cosmology as a paradigm for describing this type of development. The laws of physics in general, and Einstein's equations of the general theory of relativity in particular, describe the development of the universe *ex nihilo*. At the moment of creation, the universe is concentrated in a tiny point. Suddenly, an explosion occurs; the universe spreads; and galaxies, stars, and planets are created—among them, the earth.

The laws of physics seem to describe this process. I write "seem to," since this description is only theoretical and not an actual description of nature. Physics as we know it today cannot describe a universe concentrated within a point. The laws of physics known to us cannot describe matter or energy concentrated in a very small volume and comprising enormous energy. In other words, the stage of the creation of the universe, the "first moment," or to be precise the range of time approaching "zero," lies outside the field of modern physics. Nevertheless, we are able to describe a certain stage of the development of a world as run by the laws of physics. This stage includes neither the "first moment" nor the present reality, when man's free choice influences development, in addition to the laws of physics.

Thus we cannot describe the stage of the evolution of life as a mere derivative of the laws of nature. To aptly describe this stage in the development of the world, we can use *human life* as a paradigm. During his lifetime, man makes many decisions based on his free will, while the laws of physics, chemistry, and biology are kept as well. This paradigm assumes the concept of creation *ex nihilo*, or change due to the activity of an external factor. As we saw above (1.7; 2.7–9), *ex nihilo* is a phenomenological concept that ignores the essence of things, their metaphysics. A rational explanation assumes the activity of an "external" factor that supervises overall development—divine providence. "When we use the word *nihilo* [*ayin* in Hebrew] we must recall that we do it for convenience of speech only. Because before creation, there was *being* [*yesh* in Hebrew]—the Holy One, blessed be He, in the glory of His being" (R. Soloveitchik, *Ha-adam Ve-olamo*, 226).

The description of evolutionary development based on the paradigm of human life is only an analogy, which can be understood in human terms. When we study all of reality and its *creative emergent* development, we conclude that instead of two paradigms, there is one and only one process of development of the world, and it takes place under divine providence. The analogy for evolutionary development that is closest to us as human beings is the life of man. We might use the first paradigm, of development following only the laws of nature, as an approximation. But this prototype is not suitable for the stage of the evolution of life. We cannot use the laws of nature alone to explain change in this stage.

10. A Conversation between an Atheist (A) and a Believer (B)

A: I will begin with a general assertion: I am an atheist. My worldview is atheism.

B: Please explain yourself. What do you mean by "atheism"?

A: I don't believe in the existence of a higher power, Divinity, or God, as you call the higher power. All of scientific development in the last centuries has proven that there is no Divinity.

B: You have made two different claims here. First, you don't believe that God exists, and second, scientific development has proved that God doesn't exist. Do you agree with me?

A: Yes.

B: At least we agree on something. Let us start with the simpler claim—belief or non-belief in God's existence. Let us give an example—freedom of choice. Most people sense their freedom of choice immediately and directly. However, we cannot prove that Mr. So-and-so has freedom of choice. Whether you or I, or anyone else in the world has freedom of choice is a question of faith. Nevertheless, most people believe absolutely in personal freedom of choice, just as most people believe absolutely in the existence of the outside world. On the other hand, let us bring an example of faith of another type. The entire world, all other people apart from myself, are characters in a dream, my dream. This is an extremely implausible belief, but we cannot prove logically that this type of belief, called "solipsism," is incorrect. The same is true for faith in God. No experiment or logical argument can prove that God exists; but on the other hand, no logic or experiment can prove that He does not exist. Immanuel Kant arrived at this conclusion very clearly. In my opinion, atheism is as implausible as solipsism. The term "atheism" belongs to the field of faith, and therefore is not a matter for proof.

A: Okay, perhaps my terminology wasn't precise enough. I agree with you that it is impossible to prove God's existence or non-existence scientifically, but you yourself noted that there are unreasonable beliefs, such as solipsism. To correct my previous formulation, I claim that recent scientific development points to the fact that faith in God is implausible. A scientist you quoted above said that Darwinism negates unnatural phenomena and causes. The theory of evolution by natural selection explains changes in the world in a manner relying solely on materialism. This theory does not require God as a creator or planner. I would say that there is a theory of evolution that explains the development of life without requiring the concept of God. This is the reason I am convinced that faith in God is unreasonable.

B: I'm glad we are not talking in terms of proof, but in terms of reasonability. I noticed that you have ignored the problem of the creation of life, which no theory explains. We cannot predict the creation of any new species, and it has been proved that no theory of evolution exists regarding the period after the creation of life (even if we do accept the fact of evolution, in light of paleontological findings). The only assumption for this proof (that the law of evolution does not exist) is that of freedom of choice.

A: I do not want to argue about the existence or non-existence of the law of evolution. Let's appeal to common sense. No man has seen God, and therefore it is completely unreasonable to explain something as having been caused by God.

B: This is a misdirected claim. Many people have, and have had, religious experiences, during which they felt God directly. "There is religious factuality, just as there is scientific factuality. There is religious reality, just as there is scientific reality" (R. Soloveitchik, "*U-bikashtem mi-sham*," 133). The Bible describes myriad experiences of connection between man and God.

A: I haven't had any such experiences, and I don't believe in them.

B: You yourself chose this topic. Let's turn to our daily experiences, and look at the natural world and its pinnacle of complexity, man. His hereditary material, the DNA, includes information that could fill many books. This is only information about his body, not about his soul. Common sense says that there must be a Creator of such a complex and delicate mechanism, that we cannot compare it with anything that man himself is capable of creating. When we look at the most simple of machines, we have no doubt that someone created it. How much more so should we assume a Creator of such a complex phenomenon as man!

In order to justify atheistic claims that there is no creator of reality, including ourselves, we must show how a creation is capable of being created without a creator. In the past, researchers thought that they had a theory—the law of evolution—that directs the development of all life from the simplest organism to man. However, we noted that Popper, Monod, and others, have proved that no such law exists. We cannot suspect any of these scientists of having theist tendencies. We conclude that the burden of proof falls on atheism itself. The atheist must explain how such a complicated creation can be created without a Creator. An ordinary person cannot fulfill such a mission at all, but extensive knowledge leads to the opposite conclusion: there is no natural law directing evolution. Divine supervision of the development of life may explain the creation of life and man. I admit that this is a matter of faith. It is impossible to explain evolution through a natural law, as no such law exists. There is, however, the fact of creative emerging development.

The concept of creation presumes formation *ex nihilo*, or change due to the operation of an external factor. We must choose between two possible explanations: the phenomenological explanation, which does not address the essence of the concept of *ex nihilo*; or the rational explanation, which assumes the existence of an "outside" factor that supervises and acts on the general development. This "outside" factor is divine providence. At any rate, the rationality of this explanation does not make it a proof. Faith remains faith, and in the metaphysical realm, there are no proofs. The faith of the believing man is absolute. He believes in the Creator, immediately and unequivocally, just as you believe in the existence of an outside world and your own personal freedom of choice.

A: I have no further reasons, but you haven't convinced me to become religious. I remain an atheist.

B: I do not intend to convert you. I only want to demonstrate that the atheist approach is by no means obvious, and a foundation for it using scientific tools is mission impossible.

Chapter Four

History

"Everything is foreseen, yet freedom of choice is given." (Ethics of the Fathers 3:19)

1. Introduction

In this chapter, we will discuss the question of the existence of laws and trends in historical development. Of course the expression "law of history" does not imply "law" in the sense used in jurisprudence; it refers to patterns of regularity in historical developments.

Does a *law of history* exist? We have already discussed the question of laws of biological, evolutionary development. We can apply the answer we found there to the domain of history, and make the assertion that there are no laws that underlie the evolution of history. However, this comparison does not offer a full explanation of the topic. We cannot condense such an important and emotionally loaded topic into two sentences. In the Western hemisphere, secular people are educated to believe in historical regularity. The existence of historical laws seems obvious. This tradition is rooted in the religious traditions of Judaism and Christianity (although in a distorted way); it also has roots in Greek philosophy, and mainly in German philosophy of the eighteenth and nineteenth centuries (Hegel, Marx, and Engels).

Marx and Engels claimed they had discovered the laws of development of human society. Based on these laws, they claimed they could predict the future of humanity. They founded their claim on analysis of the first stage of capitalism (so-called "unrestrained capitalism"). I will not analyze the works of Marx and Engels here, just as I do not analyze other specific theories. I am not dealing here with science, but with *metascience*—the science of sciences. Metascience aspires to understand the logical structure of science. Marxism, the theory of Marx, Engels, and their followers, had a strong influence on broad strata of the Western intelligentsia for long periods of time. Even after the fall of the Soviet empire and the failure of the predictions of Marx and Engels, their theories still have a certain influence (largely subconscious).

Recently, I saw a television interview of a professor who specializes in a certain field of Judaism. He has researched this topic for several decades, though he does not believe in anything that he researches (at least, that is what he claims). In an aside, he mentioned "inherent historical laws." Herein lies the root of the problem. From the materialistic point of view, history is the continuation of the development of nature; it is the continuation of biological, evolutionary development. Therefore, regularity in history depends on the laws of nature. Today, the materialistic viewpoint is still widespread amongst scientists in the natural sciences as well as in the humanities. Of course, I disagree with the materialistic conception of human history. Before going into a detailed analysis of this topic, I will quote the astute words of F. Fukuyama:

> Today, everybody *talks* about human dignity, but there is no consensus as to why people possess it. Certainly few people believe that man is dignified because he is capable of moral choice. The entire thrust of modern natural science and philosophy since the time of Kant and Hegel has been to deny the possibility of autonomous moral choice, and to understand human behavior entirely in terms of sub-human and sub-rational impulses. What

once appeared to Kant as free and rational choice was seen by Marx as the product of economic forces, or by Freud as deeply hidden sexual urges. According to Darwin, man literally evolved from the subhuman; more and more of what he was was understandable in terms of biology and biochemistry. The social sciences in this century have told us that man is a product of his social and environmental conditioning, and that human behavior like animal behavior operates according to certain deterministic laws.... Modern man now sees that there is a continuum from the 'living slime,' as Nietzsche put it, all the way up to himself; he was different quantitatively but not qualitatively from the animal life out of which he came.... Man's superior dignity entitles him to conquest of nature...made possible through modern natural science. But modern natural science seems to demonstrate that there is no essential difference between man and nature, that man is simply a more organized and rational form of slime. (*The End of History and the Last Man*, 297)

2. There Is No Law-Based Regularity in History

Now I will return to the reasoning I employed in earlier sections (2.5, 3.5) where we showed that we cannot use logical reasoning to infer theory from experiment, despite the prevalent opinion of laymen and scientists. David Hume came to this conclusion in the eighteenth century. In Hume's footsteps, Kant decreed that there are a priori assumptions that are not inferred from experience, and that constitute the basis of science. In the twentieth century, Popper developed his theory of scientific cognition whereby all the sciences are deductive and are inferred logically from certain basic assumptions. According to Popper, these basic premises are human creations. (Note that in chapter 2, I demonstrated that they are divine revelations.)

Although we cannot infer a theory from observation and experiment, we can test a theory through its experimental ramifications. We can strengthen the theory by applying it to other experiments, and most importantly—we must be able to disprove the theory through experiment. We cannot prove the theory (to do this, we would need an infinite number of experiments), but we can negate it by a limited number of experiments, or even one single experiment. A theory that we cannot test experimentally is not scientific; it is metaphysical.

We will now ask ourselves whether we can, based on historical data, construct a scientific theory of history, or determine "laws" governing history. Clearly, the scientist must test any law with new experiments in order to corroborate or negate it. However, the historian has only a limited number of historical facts at his disposal. He cannot test his theory with new experiments; all he has is a historical record, the history of mankind. The historian is also incapable of refuting his own theory, since he needs a new experiment for that, too. Karl Popper speaks of the limits of experimental inquiry into natural laws:

> [I]t is clear that any law, formulated in this or in any other way, must be *tested* by new instances before it can be taken seriously by science. But we cannot hope to test a universal hypothesis nor to find a natural law acceptable to science if we are for ever confined to the observation of one unique process. Nor can the observation of one unique process help us to foresee its future development. (*The Poverty of Historicism*, 109)

Clearly, this argument that is true for the laws of nature is also true for the discipline of history. Some say that history follows a trend. They believe in progress (we will ignore the problem of defining this concept). Faith in an absolute trend, such as progress in history, has nothing in common with science. The claim of an absolute trend is metaphysical. To those who believe in historical trends, the deviations from the trend (like the regimes of Hitler or Stalin) do not contradict the trend. In other words, facts that deviate from the trend do not negate the claim that the trend exists. They can always say that in the long run, deviations in opposing directions will straighten the line. Popper has carried out a detailed analysis of the lack of law-based regularity in human history in *The Open Society and Its Enemies* (vol. 1: Plato; vol. 2: Hegel and Marx) and *The Poverty of Historicism*.

3. The Influence of the Level of Human Knowledge on Historical Developments

The title of this section seems to contradict the thesis that there are no laws of history. I will respond to this claim later. First I will focus on the connection between human knowledge and human living conditions. In order to understand this connection, we will return to Popper's three worlds (2.5). Apart from the two worlds—world one, the material world, and world two, our inner world—we identify an additional world, that of objective knowledge, such as science, mathematics, philosophy, theology, art, and so on.

Our lives are dependent on world three, its state and the level of its objective knowledge. I am using the word *knowledge* intentionally, since its meaning is more general than *science*. We can use the term *knowledge* for all stages of human history, while the term *science* is more suitable for modern science, which began in the seventeenth century. (Here I am using the word *science* in the contemporary sense; Maimonides uses this word in a different way.) Various objects of world one, such as books and electronic gadgets, document the objective knowledge of world three. In the past, a tradition passed down orally in a mimetic manner through the generations preserved objective knowledge. Nowadays, too, a large amount of information is stored in world two. This is why schools of thought are so important—they are a modern version of the oral tradition.

We have difficulty imagining the conditions of human life with a low level of objective knowledge. It would be inaccurate to compare this way of life with that of animals. Animals have a complex system of instincts, which is their objective knowledge. They pass on this genetic knowledge from generation to generation. Their world three is the DNA, which acts as a biological agent.

As an example, let us examine a native African tribe. Careful study of the tribe shows that its members have transmitted a great deal of knowledge from father to son and from mother to daughter. We might say that man's very existence depends on world three, the world of objective knowledge. When we compare the living conditions of primitive tribes to our standard of living, we might get the impression that progress is only of a material character. However, it is not so.

The spiritual dimension of man is the reservoir of his knowledge of religion, morality, philosophy, and art. The spiritual dimension of the Jew lies first of all in the Bible, the Talmud, the midrash, *halakhah*, and Jewish philosophy. It means that general culture is understood through the prism of Judaism.

A lack of awareness of Judaism's spiritual dimension sometimes leads to erroneous interpretations of the biblical text. The biblical account of the act of creation gives no details describing the process. The Omnipotent God plans different stages of creation, but the Bible does not explain how He put the plan into action. "God said, 'let there be light,' and there was light" (Genesis 1:3). This leads many to claim that Torah is incompatible with science. Yet even on the human scale, when a great scientist invents a theory, years can pass from the lightning moment of the theory's conception to its implementation. Another example: when a talented composer writes a composition, its first performance may be many years down the road. The book of Genesis describes the planning of creation, but not its implementation.

In addition to material knowledge in world three, the world of objective knowledge, we are graced with spiritual knowledge. We have identified two types of objective knowledge—material and spiritual. The two types of knowledge affect our lives in fundamentally different ways. God revealed the Torah to the Jews, and through them He transmitted a moral message to all of mankind—what is good and what is bad. This moral message does not force people to perform certain acts or refrain from others. As it is said in Ethics of the Fathers (see the quote at the start of this chapter), we have what is termed *reshut*, which means free will or freedom of choice (literally, "permission"). This freedom of choice spans the depraved evil and the extreme good. Thousands of years have passed since the Torah was given on Mount Sinai, yet in the twentieth century we have witnessed atrocities of incomparable scale. On the other hand, figures from our distant past, such as Abraham and Moses, serve as eternal moral models for all humanity.

Part of world three contains objective spiritual knowledge. Here we must add a reservation. We said above (1.5) that the word *objective* does not necessarily point to the truth of the content. It points to the independence of world three from individual opinion. The material type of objective knowledge is completely unrelated to ethics. This knowledge contributes to society's material advancement. Here, freedom of choice plays a minor role. The invention of the wheel brought general material progress, independently of individual desire. Material objective knowledge (as opposed to spiritual objective knowledge, the term we will use below) eventually influences a large proportion of human society. Another important aspect of this knowledge is its cumulative effect. Over time, with the growth of material knowledge, society's standard of living goes up.

In the last few centuries, modern science has entered the body of objective knowledge. We noted before (2.1) the influence of science on population growth (Leibowitz, *Conversations about Science and Values*). Here we will depict this influence in graphic form. In the first century CE, the population of the world numbered about four hundred million, while in the middle of the eighteenth century CE, it was around seven hundred fifty million. Thus the population doubled itself in about two thousand years, or about seventy generations. This means that most generations did not increase the population. Yet in the twelve generations since the eighteenth century, the population has grown seven times. Indeed, scientific thought existed before the eighteenth century, but the application of the results of scientific endeavors to human life began only two hundred years ago. The following graph shows the influence of the implementation of science on worldwide population growth.

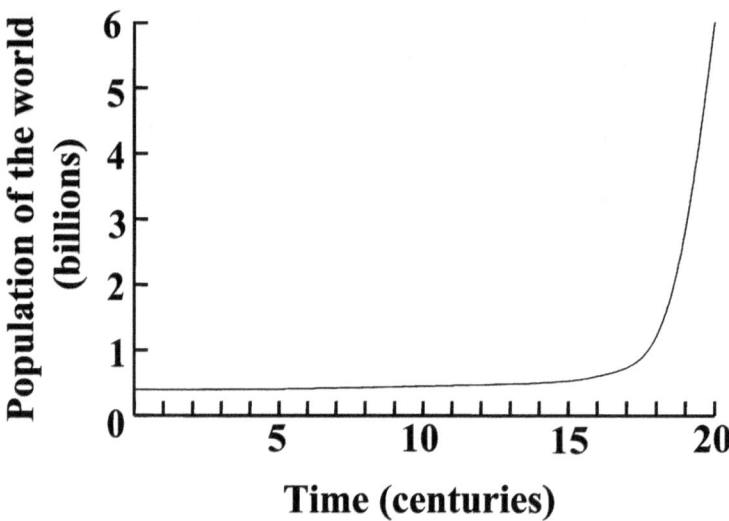

In the seventeenth and eighteenth centuries, the Jewish population numbered less than a million people. The Jewish population growth has increased at a much faster rate than world population growth. In 1939, before the Holocaust, the Jewish population was about eighteen million people. This means that the growth of the Jewish population at that time was four times faster than world population growth! If we were dealing with metaphysical speculation here, we might say that this is evidence of divine intervention.

We may now formulate the conclusion of this section: *the growth of human knowledge, both material and spiritual, influences the process of human history.* World three, of both material and spiritual objective knowledge, influences each individual person as well as human history. In other words, man's inner world, world two, is anchored in world three, and human development depends on development in world three. This brings us to a critical question: What drives development in world three? Popper answers that world three is man-made. This answer is appropriate for the worldview that places man at the center of the universe, but this worldview gives only a partial answer, and the question remains as to the source of the knowledge he uses to fill world three.

In chapter 2 of this book, in the context of scientific development, we confronted the problem of how new knowledge is created. A brief answer: the creation of scientific knowledge is an *ex nihilo* creation, the revelation of God. In fact, new knowledge is *ex nihilo* only from our point of view. From a more general point of view, there is no *ex nihilo*, but rather the creation of man whose mind is connected with the divine intellect and whose knowledge ultimately comes from God. On this we have quoted Maimonides (*Guide of the Perplexed* 1:1): "Man possesses as his proprium [nature] something in him that is very strange as it is not found in anything else that exists under the sphere of the moon, namely, intellectual apprehension.... It was because of this something, I mean *because of the divine intellect conjoined with man*, that it is said of the latter that he is 'in the image of God and in His likeness'" (*Guide of the Perplexed* 1:1; emphasis mine). An intellectual achievement, expressed in a contribution to a body of new knowledge, is *ex nihilo* from man's point of view when we distance ourselves from God. But the mystery disappears from the *ex nihilo* when we consider that God has endowed man with aspects of the divine intellect.

Up till now, we have spoken of intellectual achievement in the realm of the laws of nature. In the case of new spiritual knowledge, the situation becomes more complex. We can test the laws of nature by experiments (but cannot verify them). On the other hand, moral laws have a completely different character. They do not determine what *is*, but what *has to be*. They constitute a moral injunction that man can choose to obey or to ignore. Here we identify the humanistic approach, according to which man decides for himself what is good and what is bad—man determines his own moral code. Again, we arrive at the viewpoint of man as the center of the universe.

But this approach, that of moral autonomy, is inconsistent. In contrast to the laws of nature, we cannot test varied and contradictory moral injunctions through experiment. Paradoxically, however much empathy we have towards Western humanism, its base is no more solid than communist or even fascist morality. In contrast, the Jewish approach maintains that God has transmitted the moral norms of *halakhah* to man, and that they are the revelation of God. But some Jewish philosophers claim that man has an independent morality, together with the divine injunction. We will discuss this in the following section.

4. Divine Injunction and Human Morality (?)

Let us redefine the problem. While one approach identifies the source of morality in divine injunction, a conflicting approach claims that man has independent, autonomous morality, existing side by side with the divine injunction.

First of all, we will discuss the reasonability of the assumption of independent morality. Avi Sagi surveys a number of Jewish sources and arrives at an unequivocal conclusion: "The central stream in Jewish literature adopts the theory of moral autonomy" (*Judaism: Between Religion and Ethics*, 270). We will analyze two sources that allegedly support the autonomy of morality.

Regarding the verse "You will be holy" (Lev. 19:2), Nachmanides writes:

> Man may commit all the vile deeds that are not prohibited in the Torah, and thus become *a miscreant within the permissible realm of the Torah*.... And such is the way of the Torah, that after it lists certain specific prohibitions, it includes them all in a general precept. Thus after warning with detailed laws regarding all business dealings between people, such as not to steal or rob or to wrong one another, He said in general, "And you shall do what is right and

good" [Deut. 6:18], thus including under a positive commandment the duty of doing that which is right and agreeing to a compromise [when not to do so would be inequitable] as well as of acting with a *measure of leniency* for the sake of pleasing his fellow humans... (Emphasis mine)

What is Nachmanides saying here? Can a Jew really observe all the 613 commandments, yet remain *a miscreant within the permissible realm of the Torah*? The point is that beyond specific commandments, the Torah educates us towards a certain pattern of behavior. In addition to fulfilling commandments, a Jew must behave according to this pattern. "And you shall do what is right and good in God's eyes" means not only must we fulfill the law, but we must also know when to act beyond the letter of the law. These are the rules of Jewish morality. It would be artificial to separate the "ethics of the commandments" from a general Jewish morality that merits being called "natural, independent morality." Independent of what? Of the Torah? The Torah is the source of "you shall do what is right and good in God's eyes," and the law is the source of "acting with a measure of leniency."

In the second source Abraham argues with God about the destruction of Sodom: "Far be it from You to do after this manner, to slay the righteous with the wicked; and that the righteous should be as the wicked, far it from You: Shall not the Judge of all the earth do justly?" (Genesis 18:25). We might argue that the very existence of such an argument proves Abraham's innate, independent morality. Only a person with a solid moral position of his own can enter into an argument with God. Yet in fact, this argument does not prove the existence of an *independent, natural morality*. Abraham's moral stance is not independent, but is *derived from his continual connection to God*. In order to understand this, we have only to compare Abraham's morality to that of his neighbors. If we find this comparison too difficult, we can compare it to that of our neighbors, or with the morality of my biological homeland, where millions, both righteous and sinners, were offered up on the altars of idolatry.

The biblical episode of the binding of Isaac clearly demonstrates that God's word is the only thing that determines Abraham's behavior. Abraham does not have his own criteria for measuring the "morality" of God's command. Whatever God commands is moral. All Abraham has to do is ensure that this is God's word, and he was indeed confident of this.

We can easily argue that the source of Jewish morality is the Torah, either directly or indirectly. However, what about the period before the giving of the Torah at Mt. Sinai? Here we find disagreements among rabbis. R. Aharon Lichtenstein believes that then, as now, man had an innate, natural quality of morality (in Fox, *Modern Jewish Ethics*, 64). He points out that God punished both Cain and the generation of the Flood for their deeds, even though the Torah did not explicitly specify the commandments for moral behavior they were required to follow. Maimonides argues the opposite (*Laws of Kings*, 80:9)—that the commandments God gave to Adam and Noah are written in the Torah. In any case, "Man was created in the image of God. A spark of the Creator was hidden in him" (R. Soloveitchik, "*U-bikashtem mi-sham*," 154). Thus we see that man does have moral responsibility, even if the Torah does not command him in writing. Indeed, only a chosen few are aware of this responsibility, so long as morality is not institutionalized. It is precisely this institutionalization of morality that is the aim of the Torah, and the mission of the Jewish people.

However, we will ignore for now both prehistory and early history, and jump forward to the present. Man is born, raised, and educated in a certain society. His soul is anchored in the particular world three of spirituality. This world three could be communist ideology (which half the world believed until recently). It could be a world three of Nazi lies, of Christianity, or Islam, of secular humanism, or of mixed religious and secular cultures. In most cases, the world three in which a person is born and grows up influences his soul. Only in isolated cases can the soul liberate itself from the trap of a false world three, as we will demonstrate in the photograph below. This photo shows a group of scientists who took part in an unauthorized scientific seminar that was illegal in the eyes of the Soviet authorities who pursued and even harassed the participants. We might ask a typical question: what is unusual about the photo (aside from the fact that only one participant is a woman)? The answer is that all the people in it are Jews, except for one—Andrei Sakharov.

Moscow 1977. In the picture, standing from right to left: Nahum Meiman, Benjamin Levich, Mark Azbel, Benjamin Fain, Andrei Sakharov, Victor Brailovsky, and Jacob Alpert. Sitting: Solomon Alber, Arkady Zinober, Irina Brailovsky.

Sakharov is not a Jew; he is a non-Jewish Russian (the Sakharov Gardens at the entrance to Jerusalem are named after him, in honor of his significant contribution to the Jewish national movement in the Soviet Union.) Andrei Sakharov's life was an outstanding example of liberating the soul from the trap of the Soviet world three. Formerly, Sakharov, a first-class scientist and physicist, and an honest man, believed in the dogmas of the regime. Not only did he believe, he also contributed, as "the father of the Soviet hydrogen bomb." At a certain point, Sakharov became aware of the regime's lies and was transformed into its fierce opponent. The weight of his authority served him well in the battle against the regime. All the scientists in the picture are, in their own way, examples of liberation from a world three of falsity, but unlike the others, the Russian scientist did not belong to a persecuted national minority, and so his rebellion is more exceptional.

We explained above that a spiritual world three is objective, but can be very far removed from the truth. The ethical systems of communism, Nazism, and extremist Islamic movements and those of various humanistic movements are entirely different. But is not the moral truth unique? The answer is that the Jewish system of morality is different from the others, in that it represents God's word. This is clear to all who were born into Judaism and educated as traditional Jews. However, to a non-Jew or to a Jew educated outside a Torah framework, this answer may seem unreasonable, even racist. This is a good reason to devote additional space to this topic.

5. Why Jews?

A special status attaches to Jews, as indicated by the biblical terminology *am segulah*, or chosen/treasured people. It is clear to many that what happens in Israel, or is connected to Jews anywhere in the world, draws the attention of the whole world, with no relevance to its importance. "Jews is news." The number of Jewish Nobel Prize winners in the sciences is out of all proportion to their relative number within the world population. The Jews' suffering is also extraordinary. These characteristics reflect the Jews' uniqueness. We will try to understand this phenomenon.

First of all, we must identify an undeniable truth: Jewish thought has had considerable influence on world culture.

1. The Jews have bequeathed the idea of monotheism to humanity.
2. The Bible (that is, the Torah) has provided the foundation for the moral systems of the great world religions ("great" according to

number of believers)—Christianity and Islam. The moral systems of these religions are not identical to Jewish morality. We cannot logically prove the truth of Jewish morality. Neither can we prove God's word; this is a matter of faith. Clearly we must use logic as much as possible. However, as we saw in chapter 2 on science, logic has limited use. Even scientific theories are merely beliefs that are tested in reality, and are somewhat corroborated by experiment. In this, they are different from arbitrary beliefs, which are not tested at all. Just as scientific theories (which are really divine revelations, as discussed in chapter 2) undergo the test of reality, so do the beliefs documented in the Bible. They influence and change the world, and we are witness to this.
3. The fact that the forces of evil have never ceased to persecute the Jews testifies to the positiveness of Jewish values. To this day, these forces still aspire to destroy the Jews, both physically and spiritually. *Evil is the antithesis of Judaism.*
4. We have already noted that science has a decisive role in historical development, and science develops within a culture based on Jewish philosophy.

Below is an explanation of the first two points. We will devote the next chapter to explicating point 4. Clause 3 demands more detailed clarification, which we will give in one of the ensuing sections.

The Jewish people make up only one-fifth of one percent of the world population today. However, their spiritual influence over the world is enormous, out of all proportion to the number of Jews. As the Bible states: "Not on account of your being a majority of all peoples did God desire you and choose you, as you are the minority of all peoples" (Deuteronomy 7:7). To influence spiritually is the main mission of the Jewish people, singling them out from all other peoples. As the Bible says, "You will be for Me a treasure from all peoples, as all the land is mine; you will be for me a kingdom of priests, and a holy nation" (Ex. 19:5–6); "I am the Lord Your God who separated you from the nations" (Lev. 20:24); "You will be holy for Me, as I am a holy God and I will separate you from the people to be for Me" (ibid., 20:26).

6. Science and Jewish Civilization

In *The End of History*, Fukuyama looks for a mechanism that explains the "directionality" of history. He concludes that the modern natural sciences are the mechanism behind this directionality. Science has a cumulative character, which allows it to influence history. In section 3, we saw in graph form how the development of science influences world population growth. However, what is the driving force, what is the meaning behind the scientific drive for research? As Einstein said, "You will hardly find one among the profounder sort of scientific minds without a religious feeling of his own…" (*Ideas and Opinions*, 49).

What is the connection between the development of science and Jewish culture, which is based on the books of the Bible? Even if we agree with Einstein that religious motivation is vital to fundamental research, we still must define the relation of this research to Judaism.

In the two thousand years since the canonization of the Bible, its perspective has had an enormous influence on the modern world. The rapid development of the natural sciences in Europe began in the seventeenth century. Why did this science develop only in Europe, in a Western environment, and not in China or India, for example, which hosted ancient civilizations? Alfred Whitehead, a well-known English mathematician and philosopher, thought that this was not by chance, but that only in the bosom of a Judeo-Christian culture could the natural sciences develop. Only a culture based on the Bible could serve as the breeding ground for scientific research.

Before we analyze his claim, we should note that in fact, he refers to Jewish civilization. When Whitehead spoke about the Bible, he meant the Christian Bible as well (of which a significant part is, of course, a translation of Jewish Scripture), but the unique contribution to the scientific world viewpoint that he identifies is derived from the Jewish Bible. Against this we might argue that for centuries, no Jews worked seriously in the natural sciences. But at that time, Jews were to a great extent banned from these pursuits. In any case, our topic here is not the scientists themselves, but the foundations of a viewpoint that stems from the Bible.

Metaphysics precedes physics. A certain worldview underlies basic science. In section 2.7, we discussed the Jewish view of scientific cognition. These are the foundations of the Jewish perspective:

(1) God created the world; such a world has unity.
(2) Creation, as described in the Torah, is the process of the appearance of order from chaos. God created order in a uniform manner for the whole world. The laws that govern the earth are identical to the laws governing the sun and the most distant galaxies.
(3) The world can be perceived and understood. This is a necessary condition for scientific research. Science cannot exist if we cannot perceive the laws of nature, even if they do exist. On the other hand, we cannot logically infer from the laws of science and nature the possibility of understanding the world, or of perceiving its laws. In the framework of scientific thought, this remains a mystery. As Albert Einstein wrote, "The eternal mystery of the world is its comprehensibility.... The fact that it is comprehensible is a miracle" (*Ideas and Opinions*, 285): Understanding the world is a basic metaphysical premise that is beyond science, beyond physics. Rather, the perspective of Torah underlies this comprehension.

These are Jewish metaphysical ideas, upon which science rests. As to the timing of the stages of development of science, this depends on divine providence. This is one of the channels through which divine providence operates.

7. Evil Is the Antithesis of Judaism

We have just presented our basic belief that the Jewish people has a mission in history. The realization of this mission involves clashes with other nations, and is the cause of anti-Semitism in the metaphysical plane (rationally, anti-Semitism has no explanation, as we will discuss below). The wonder of the survival of the Jewish people, a people subject to the constant hostility of the nations of the world, can be explained only through divine intervention. "It is this promise that has sustained our ancestors und us, for not just one enemy has arisen to destroy us; rather in every generation there are those who seek our destruction, but the Holy One, praised be He, saves us from their hands" (*Passover Haggadah*, The Rabbinical Assembly, 1982).

It is well known that hatred of Jews is an emotion with no rational explanation, defying ordinary logic. However, one of the historical characteristics of anti-Semitism is that Jew-haters are always on the side of evil. In this context, the American novelist Sinclair Lewis wrote: "There is no greater compliment to the Jews than the fact that the degree of their unpopularity is always the scientific measure of the cruelty and silliness of the régime under which they live..." (*It Can't Happen Here*, 293). The present era has a special status in the history of mankind, since the Holocaust occurred during this period. Philosophers such as Emil Fackenheim, Eli Wiesel, and Shalom Rosenberg are of the opinion that the Holocaust embodied an evil that was essentially different, that cannot be explained logically. The Holocaust was, in the words of Shalom Rosenberg, "the revelation of evil, an almost mystical evil with unparalleled cosmic dimensions, that led to uncompromising depravity,...a kind of antithesis to the giving of the Torah; we must study this phenomenon which has changed our lives totally" (*Good and Evil in Jewish Philosophy*, 83).

During every epoch, Jews have suffered persecutions, but in the twentieth and twenty-first centuries, the mobilization of the nations of the world against the Jews has reached new heights. The Holocaust took place in the twentieth century. The absolute evil of Nazism is, beyond any shadow of a doubt, the antithesis of Judaism.

In this context, we should clarify man's measure of responsibility for doing evil. God created man and gave him freedom of will. He transmitted to man the responsibility for doing good or bad. Divine providence takes place "behind the scenes"; man can neither understand nor explain it. But man retains free will and responsibility for his deeds. If God were to revoke freedom of choice, then man could not do evil. However, then he would not be a man, but a robot or a puppet. This is not the kind of world that God wanted to create. "I am the Lord, and there is none else, I form the light, and create darkness; I make peace and create evil: I, the Lord do all these things" (Isaiah 45:6–7).

Here we will try to ignore the metaphysical plane and to discuss the human factor. In the end, man bears all responsibility for his deeds. We will therefore discuss the issue that is disturbing us: the evil deeds of anti-Semites. Although this is an age-old problem, we will confine ourselves to representatively examining the roles of various peoples in the most egregious anti-Semitic persecution in history, the Second World War.

1. *Nazi Germany.* Nazi Germany is responsible for the evil of the regime that it created and for the destruction of six million Jews.
2. *The States of Occupied Eastern Europe.* Ukrainians, Lithuanians, Hungarians, Poles, Latvians, and other peoples supported Germany and participated in its acts of atrocity. Their participation in the Germans' monstrous deeds turned them into *totally evil people,* even though some were evil beforehand as well.
3. *The Allies.* (Here I rely on Eliezer Berkowitz's *Faith after the Holocaust.*) Often we hear that the Allies were indifferent to the Nazi evil. However, their attitude went beyond apathy to sabotage of any efforts to save the Jews. Before the German authorities put their Final Solution into place, when the Jews still had a chance to emigrate, the Allied countries closed the ports of the Land of Israel

and America to Jewish immigration. At the beginning of the 1980s, I heard a lecture at Oxford based on material released for publication after forty years of secret classification. These documents revealed that heads of a number of Eastern European states approached the British government asking to allow the Jews of their lands to immigrate to Mandate Palestine. These heads of governments realized that the anticipated German invasion meant the death sentence for the Jews in their countries. After a discussion with his advisors, Winston Churchill refused to allow the Jews of these countries to enter the Mandate Palestine. His excuse was that the immigrants might include Nazi agents. This act of Churchill's negated all his previous gestures towards the Jews. As for the US State Department, it did what it could to prevent information about Nazi crimes from reaching America, lest this information inflame public opinion there.

For much of the period during which the destruction of the Jews of Europe took place, the Allies published no official document condemning the horrific acts of Nazi Germany. The Moscow Declaration of 1943, which warned the Nazis about their responsibilities, mentioned many war crimes, but said nothing about the Jews, the focal point of German hatred. Such a policy indisputably encouraged Germany to continue implementing their Final Solution to the "Jewish problem." Many Western countries shared German anti-Semitism, as anti-Semitism had deep roots in Christian culture. It is true that Nazi ideology had nothing in common with Christianity. But the Nazis were products of some two thousand years of Christian culture. The German Nazis absorbed the spirit of intolerance, hatred, jealousy, and degradation towards Jews that prevailed in Europe throughout the Christian millennia.

4. *The Soviet Union:* The Soviet Union sided with the Allies during WWII, and shared their attitude toward the Jews. However, the Soviet Empire had its own individual version of this attitude, reflected in the past of Czarist Russia with its tradition of anti-

Jewish pogroms. The Soviet Union is unique in that tens of millions of innocent citizens died in a violent struggle over a "radiant future," while at the same time millions of people suffered in the Gulag camps (the Soviet concentration camps.)

After WWII, the Soviet Union continued its battle against the Jews. Before the war, the battle was against Judaism as a religion, but afterward, it became a battle against any signs of Jewishness, against everything Jewish. Anti-Semitism became governmental policy. If the aim of Nazi Germany was the physical destruction of the Jews, then the aim of the Soviet Union was complete spiritual destruction. The two cases of Nazi Germany and Soviet Russia clearly demonstrate that *evil is the antithesis of Judaism.* At the end of the 1980s and the beginning of the nineties, the Soviet Empire collapsed. How can we not see the revelation of God's will in this?!

The twentieth century was witness to an event of such importance that we can evaluate it only from the perspective of time. I refer to the establishment of the State of Israel. Imagine a person who lived centuries ago traveling to the mid-twentieth century through a magic time machine. We can picture this time-traveler observing an infinite number of amazing things—cars, planes, radio, television, and more. The biggest surprise of all awaits him when he studies the maps of the world—the State of Israel! Everything else that the time-traveler sees has a natural explanation, but here no explanation is adequate. Here we are speaking about another plane, beyond human logic—this is divine providence.

Then in 1967, the world was again put to the test. Twenty-two years after the end of the Second World War, the tiny State of Israel faced great danger. The Arabs swore to wipe the state off the face of the earth, and to throw the Jews into the sea. The world was definitely ready to accept this. Statesmen, religious leaders, the church—all were apathetically silent. The conscience of the world prepared to digest the new tragedy, just as it digested Hitler's death camps. However, the Arabs made a mistake in their calculations, and their hopes were dashed. Nevertheless, the nations of the world took no part in Israel's salvation; the Jews simply knew now how to defend themselves.

Again, we are discussing "evil as the antithesis to Judaism." The evil of Nazi Germany and Soviet Russia is total. The fact that those representing evil declared war on Jews and Judaism is the fulfillment of this concept. This is as clear as black and white. However, the anti-Semitism of the postwar Western world is generally hidden, disguised as anti-Zionist and anti-Israel policy. The new anti-Semites present Arab terrorists, murderers of innocent men, women, and children as "freedom fighters," their victims as the "aggressors."

However, not all the world stands against us. The subtleties are important here, as is the measure of anti-Semitism. The policy of many Western European countries is dictated first of all by egotistical interests, not by principles, and their attitude toward the State of Israel comprises a mixture of anti-Semitism and anti-Zionism. The policy of the United States, however, is different, since it takes a more principled stance with respect to morality. Not by chance has America remained the only superpower, and at the same time the only friend we have in the world.

8. *Human History—Providence and Freedom of Will*

The level of objective knowledge, world three, influences human history, and this might seem to offer the possibility of determining laws that govern history (at the beginning of section 3 I promised to answer this question). However, we cannot predict changes in knowledge; therefore, we cannot determine laws for history. The impossibility of predicting change in knowledge within a known system (such as human society) stems from the concept expressed in a logical sentence proved by Karl Popper: "Self-prediction is impossible" (*The Open Universe*—see below).

From all that we have learned, we conclude that world three, the world of objective knowledge, is subject to divine providence. We find a high degree of correspondence between divine providence and the logical structure of knowledge. The fact that we cannot predict its future precisely confirms the impossibility of predicting divine providence. Accordingly, God is the One who determines the development of world three, and He is the One who directs human history. Nevertheless, He is not the only contributor to the historical process. Man is God's partner in history; he has freedom of will. R. Soloveitchik describes it thus:

> The Torah, which based all of Judaism on the principle of creativity and Providence on the one hand, and the principle of Israel's being chosen on the other hand, placed the concepts of kindness and love at the very nexus of its world. The creation of the world is the manifestation of God's love. Divine Providence over all His creatures, and in particular the election of Israel, are expressions of His infinite love. Anyone who claims that man is commanded to love God, but that there is no reciprocity, rejects a fundamental tenet of Judaism. ("*U-bikashtem mi-sham*," 121, note 2)

Providence is one of the general principles of Judaism. I would like to emphasize that we are not capable of understanding how divine providence works. For example, we do not understand *how* the infinite mind connects with finite human intelligence, even though we can understand the *necessity* of this. In any case, disregarding questions of "how" which we cannot answer, we nevertheless are able to describe certain channels of providence. In modern physics, too, scientists have learned to disregard questions of "how," and this does not stand in the way of a successful description of reality.

A person is born into a certain world of culture, technology, science, religion, philosophy, and spiritual and material objective knowledge, which Karl Popper calls world three. This world of knowledge influences us; each one of us is educated within it, and without it there is no humanity. In addition to the world of general culture, there is a world of Jewish culture, philosophy, and religion, a "Jewish world three." A Jew, if he is a Jew in essence, is so not only because of circumstances of birth or conversion, but because he was educated and/or grew up in a Jewish world three, as man in general is the cultural product of a general world three.

If a Jew born to a Jewish mother is cut off from Jewish sources and traditions, as happened to the majority of the Soviet Union's Jews, he still has a Jewish identity (*who* is he?), but he does not have a Jewish essence (*what* is he?). However, this situation is not irreversible. When a Jew is exposed to a world of Jewish spiritual knowledge, he can, if he so desires, repent his deeds, and become a Jew in essence. This process can take many years. Gershom Scholem, researcher of kabbalah, was born in Germany in 1895 to an assimilated family. He wrote that joining the Zionist movement did not take him very long, but to become a Jew in essence took him more than ten years (*Devarim Be-Go, On Jews and Judaism in Crisis*).

Until now, we have considered world three of spiritual and material objective knowledge as a given fact. However, we must also understand how world three develops historically, its evolution. Here divine providence is involved: it operates on the individual, who receives prophecy or divine revelation, and thus new knowledge is created *ex nihilo*. The individual's new knowledge enters into world three and is recorded there in different ways.

Below is a diagram depicting schematically the transition that a given item of new knowledge makes. This new knowledge passes from the infinite mind, through a certain "self" and its finite mind, into world three, the world of objective knowledge. Thus, the world of objective knowledge is filled up gradually by the human being who mediates between the infinite mind and world three:

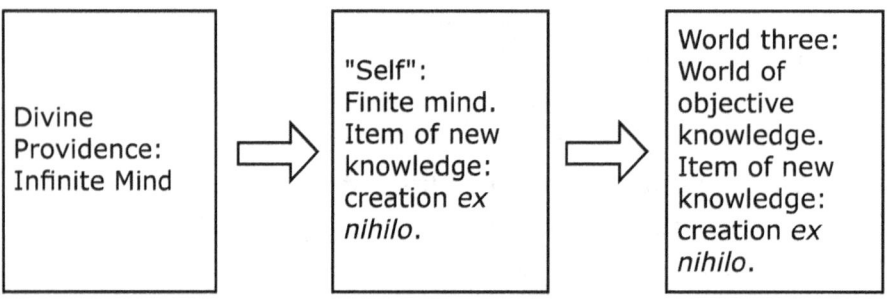

On the other hand, man enables world three to influence world one (the material world):

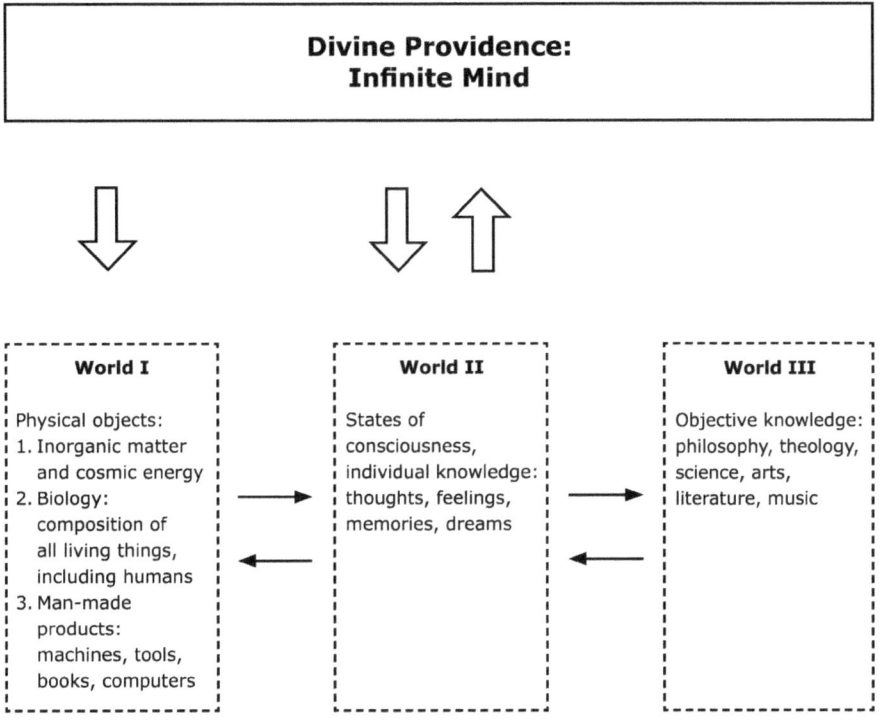

The world open to God

We will now return to the diagram in 1.5, in order to complete Karl Popper's former diagram with the concept of *openness of the world to God*. As we explained, and as shown in the first diagram above, the individual self is open to the infinite mind, and this leads to the development of world three, and the entire world in general. However, divine providence also influences world one, including the creation of the world and biological evolution on earth. Accordingly, the arrows in the diagram before us are directed to worlds one and two. Divine providence influences world three indirectly, through man. The arrow pointing upwards from world two leads to the infinite mind, indicating reciprocity between man and God.

We have already said that the infinite mind exudes a profusion of material knowledge, such as scientific theories, moral knowledge, and ethical precepts.

Let us consider again the transmission of material knowledge (d. 2002), which we discussed in section 2.9. My colleague Alvin Radkowsky, a God-fearing scientist, wrote the following in his essay "The Faith of an Orthodox Jewish Scientist Revisited":

> Still I believe that scientific discoveries must be to Divine inspiration; as Yaakov said: 'Because the Lord your G-d granted me good fortune' (*Genesis* 27:20). In my own case ideas have come to me as an experience resembling a flash of light. Invention is almost *l'havdil* [taking into account the vast differences] a sort of *neviut* [*prophecy*]. (*B'Or Ha'Torah*, 1:22)

Karl Popper, the secular philosopher and expert on the history of science, wrote in a similar vein:

> It is [the scientist's] intuition, his *mystical* insight into the nature of things, rather than his reasoning, which makes a great scientist.... Creativeness is an entirely irrational, a *mystical* faculty... (*The Open Society and Its Enemies*, vol. 2: Hegel and Marx, 228; emphasis mine)

These two quotes emphasize again the *divine source* of man's scientific knowledge.

However, man's cultural world, his world three, did not begin with science. The true drama began with the creation of man. Here we must clarify that we are not discussing the natural history of man. Such a history is based on materialist theory, and cannot describe man's *self*, which is neither a material nor a biological entity, as already emphasized in chapter 1, "Mind and Body." Moreover, the divine mind connects to man's soul. Consequently, in our search for true understanding of historical development, we must look within the spiritual plane; as our faith tells us, this means the Bible and other Jewish sources.

God created man as a partner in history and gave him freedom of choice. "God blessed them and said to them, 'Go forth and multiply and fill the earth and conquer it and you will rule the fish of the sea and the bird of the sky and every animal that crawls on the earth'" (Genesis 1:28). In order to be a *partner* with God, man must have free will. Without it, man would be like a robot that fulfills its master's will. Nevertheless, free will also creates a problem. Each person has his own will; these individual wills may conflict with each other. Free will allows each person to decide according to his understanding, or contrary to it; to hear the voice of God, or to ignore it, as Adam did in the Garden of Eden (Genesis 3).

According to the naturalistic perspective, which negates divinity, mankind includes all the varied wills of individual men, and each one has freedom of choice (here we continue to uphold the concept of freedom of choice, although this is in possible contradiction to the negation of divinity). History has no laws, and therefore we conclude that it comprises nothing but total chaos. This is the logical conclusion of the materialistic, naturalistic premise regarding the history of the human race, if it is the product of a countless number of desires without regularity or direction.

Things look completely different if we assume that the infinite mind is running and supervising human history. Indeed, we do not know how this providence intervenes, just as we do not understand how the infinite divine mind is connected to the finite human mind.

Is history the result of man's freedom of choice, or God's divine plan? This subject has occupied many generations of Jewish philosophers. Until now, we have dealt with significant issues in human history. Now we are reaching the heart of the historical problem. *Everything is foreseen, yet freedom of choice is given.* This is the meaning of historical development. Below I review various opinions on the subject including my own understanding of this concept.

9. Jewish Philosophers on "Everything is foreseen, yet freedom of choice is given"

A. Divine Providence and Freedom of Choice

Divine providence is one of the major principles of Judaism. God intervenes in man's affairs, He runs history, and He is the God of history. The first of the Ten Commandments demonstrates this: "I am the Lord your God who took you out of the Land of Egypt from the house of slavery" (Exodus 20:3). Another important principle is that God gave man freedom of choice. History is the story of God contending with humans who have freedom of choice. In the following chapters, we will focus on the problem of freedom of choice versus divine providence.

Rabbi Akiva said, "Everything is foreseen, yet freedom of choice is given." Maimonides emphasizes in his commentary on the Mishna that "this saying includes very great things, and it is worthy of Rabbi Akiva." Rabbi Akiva speaks of two great principles: Divine providence and freedom of choice. These principles seem to contradict each other radically. The first assumption, "everything is foreseen" means there is an omnipotent God who knows man's deeds in advance, and determines all man's actions from the very beginning. Thus, as Maimonides observes, "man is obligated from on High in every one of his deeds." But this contradicts the second assumption, freedom of choice.

Yet we must not give up the principle of freedom of choice. Without freedom of choice, there is no point in the *mitzvot* (God's commandments). Maimonides expresses himself on this subject decisively:

> If man were compelled in his deeds, the commandments of the Torah and its warnings would be null and void. Everything would be a complete lie, as man would have no choice in what he will do. This would require cancellation of learning and the study of all

philosophy. All of this would be foolishness and idleness. (*Eight Chapters*, chapter 8)

However, the principle of divine providence is also a vital principle of Judaism. In Rabbi Akiva's opinion, divine providence includes God's knowledge of the future, even if this knowledge prima facie contradicts freedom of choice.

We can interpret Rabbi Akiva's words as an insoluble paradox for man. Yet Jewish philosophers have attempted to solve this paradox in various ways. Below is a review of studies on the topic, among which Maimonides' contribution features prominently. Accordingly, I will begin with a description of his approach. In C, I will review the approaches of other Jewish philosophers in chronological order and in section 10, I will suggest an additional way to view this problem.

B. Maimonides' Approach to the Problem of Freedom of Choice versus Divine Knowledge

Man has complete freedom of choice. An omnipotent God knows the future, but His knowledge is different from man's knowledge. Therefore, there is no contradiction between freedom of choice, something that we know (or that we think that we know), and God's knowledge that we do not understand and are incapable of understanding. "My thoughts are not your thoughts, and My ways are not your ways" (Hoshea 53:8). Maimonides rules, "As it is so, we do not have the power to know how God knows all creatures and deeds. However, we know beyond all doubt that man's deeds are in his own hands, and God does not direct him, and does not decree for him to act in that manner" (*Laws of Repentance* 5:5).

Maimonides differentiates between man's knowledge and God's. Human thought separates between subject and object. Man (the subject) knows something about a certain fact or about another person (the object). This knowledge does not influence the object's status. Not so with God: "He is the One who knows, the known, and the knowledge itself—all is unity" (*Foundations of the Torah* 2:10). "He, may His name be blessed, is His characteristics, and his characteristics are Him, until it will be said about Him: He is knowledge, He is the One who knows and He is the known, He is the living One and He is the life, and He continues life for Himself" (*Eight Chapters*, 8). In his *Guide of the Perplexed* Maimonides explains again that God's knowledge is not in the same category as ours, so that we are not able to draw an analogy with regard to it; but His knowledge is totally different in every way (*Guide of the Perplexed* 3:20).

Let us recapitulate Maimonides' words. Man has total freedom of choice (*reshut netunah*), and the concept "everything is foreseen" (*hakol tzafui*) is transcendental and incomprehensible for us, therefore there is no contradiction between these two claims—the human mind is not able to compare them. However, Maimonides is not satisfied with this conclusion and in his momentous *Guide of the Perplexed* he sharpens the paradox yet further. If man has two possibilities, he is free to choose between them. However, God's knowledge of what will happen "does not make this possible thing quit its nature, and this constitutes a great difficulty for the apprehension of our inadequate intellects" (ibid.). He clarifies this further: "God's knowledge, may He be exalted, does not bring about the actualization of one of the two possibilities even though He, may He be exalted, knows perfectly how one of them will come about." In Y. Ben Shlomo's commentary on *Guide of the Perplexed*, he observes, "God's knowledge does not cause the realization of one of the possibilities, even though God knows exactly which of them will be realized."

Possibly, we cannot employ the concept of time in regards to God. Perhaps this is why we have difficulty understanding how God knows what will be realized. But it is also hard for us to reconcile free choice on the one hand, and necessity on the other—when all our life is a chain of decisions and choices, yet God "knows exactly which of them will be realized." Maimonides negated the possibility that God knows and does not intervene; for the divine, there is no separation between subject and object.

C. Other Jewish Philosophers

As we have said, the problem of free choice as opposed to divine foreknowledge appears in the Bible and in the Talmud. Freedom of choice is a metaphysical concept that we cannot prove in experiments; it is a matter of faith. Belief in freedom of choice permeates the entire Bible; it is an unequivocal religious certainty that the Talmud formulated in the saying "Everything is in God's hands, apart from fear of God" (Tractate Brakhot 33b.) The Jewish sages were aware of the contradiction between divine knowledge and human choice. They did not try to resolve it, but instead grasped two points of faith as one: "Everything is foreseen, yet permission (freedom of choice) is given. The world is judged with mercy, yet the verdict is according to one's deeds" (Ethics of the Fathers 3:19). In contrast to this attitude, Jewish philosophers invested great energies in trying to find a possible solution to the problem of freedom of choice and God's knowledge.

According to the determinist perspective of *Philo of Alexandria* (c. 20 BCE—50 CE), all acts attributed to created beings, including man, are in truth performed by God. According to this opinion, words of Torah were not directed towards man as a creature of free will, but for the benefit of those people who are unaware of the secret of God's greatness and His creations' insignificance.

R. Saadia Gaon (882–942) wrote that divine justice "implies two metaphysical assumptions: free will, and a belief in the hereafter. Together with belief in God, they form the three basic truths of religion: God, freedom and immortality..." (Guttmann, *Philosophy of Judaism*, 82). In contrast to the Islamic theory of predestination, R. Saadia proves that without the assumption of free will, God's commandments have no meaning. If man cannot be held responsible for his sins, then punishing him is not in line with the concept of divine justice. Moreover, R. Saadia considered freedom of choice to be an unmediated fact of consciousness, which teaches us that we ourselves determine our deeds (compare the views of Immanuel Kant, see above, 1.2.). He resolves the contradiction between God's all-encompassing knowledge and man's free will by asserting that divine knowledge is not the reason behind the freely made decisions of humanity. These are independent of God, even if God is aware of them in advance.

Clearly, this approach (which is similar to Maimonides') does not solve the problem. If all of man's deeds are known in advance, then the concept of freedom of choice loses its meaning.

Bahya ben Joseph Ibn Pekuda (Rabbeinu Bahya, eleventh century) takes the position that man cannot solve the problem of freedom of choice and God's knowledge:

> This opinion, which says that man cannot correctly solve this question, is more acceptable than others...and saves man from a mistake and false opinions in which he may fail by confusion in these issues. Truth and common sense bring about a situation that we will admit that our lack of knowledge in this matter—because of our weak intelligence and our insufficient consciousness that cannot achieve it—stems from the Creator's wisdom. Our lack of knowledge is for our own good, and therefore this matter is concealed from us. For if it would be advantageous for us to understand this secret, God would reveal it to us. (*Duties of the Heart*, "Serving God," chapter 8)

Rabbi Yehuda Halevi (1075–1141), in an approach similar to that of R. Saadia Gaon, supports the theory of man's freedom of choice. This choice is not removed from the realm of divine rule. According to R. Halevi, God is the primary cause of everything. From Him, intermediary causes evolved. According to the types of these causes, all processes divide into natural, coincidental, and arbitrary (i.e., resulting from human choice). Accordingly, human choice is not an exception to God's decree. R. Halevi recognizes the problem of freedom of choice versus God's knowledge. In his opinion, "the knowledge of events to come is not the cause of their existence" (Kuzari 5:20); however, the problem is that an event known in advance contradicts the possible character of the event. In R. Halevi's opinion, this knowledge is not limited to God's knowledge alone. "The things that we have said are correct whether we are speaking about the knowledge of the Divine or of angels, prophets or fortune tellers" (ibid.). The proof of this claim relies on the fact that otherwise we confront a paradox, the same paradox that R. Halevi was supposed to solve. "If knowledge were a cause of existence, then some people would merit Paradise because of their Divine knowledge, as they are righteous people, even if they did not serve Him. Others would be punished in Gehinnom because of His knowledge that they are sinners, even if they did not sin" (ibid.).

Like R. Halevi, *Ibn Daud, Abraham ben David* (also known as Rabad, c. 1110–1180) divides the issue into divine, natural, coincidental, and arbitrary causes. In his opinion, in some people the measure of good or bad will is so strong that they need not activate their freedom of choice at all. But most people fall between these two extremes, so they must choose between good or bad. Their choice entitles them to either reward or punishment. While other Jewish philosophers expanded God's omniscience to include man's freely chosen deeds, and said that the freedom of human decisions is not affected by God's advance knowledge of the results, the Rabad removes man's deeds from the axiom of prior divine knowledge. The Rabad bravely declares that God "limited His omniscience even as He limited His omnipotence in regard to human acts" (Guttmann, *Philosophy of Judaism*, 171). In the Rabad's words, God cannot know an event in advance "that is not pre-determined from an objective point of view."

Chronologically, Maimonides' approach should appear here (1135–1204). However, because of the importance of Maimonides' opinion on this issue, I devoted a separate section to him at the beginning of this summary.

Abner of Burgos (after converting to Christianity, he was known as Alfonso of Vallodolid, 1270–1340) tried to bring the determinist Islamic Aristotelian method of predestination into the field of Jewish thought. According to his theory, the principle of natural causality also applies to man's acts of will, just as it applies to any external occurrence. Man's decisions are not dependent on his own arbitrary will, but are a necessary result of the justifications operating on him. In essence, he decides between various possibilities, but his decision is made according to the laws of causality. Arguing logically, Abner rejects the accepted proofs against the theory of predestination. The assumption that human acts are necessary refutes no divine commandment. Reward and punishment are the necessary concomitants of human deeds, and there is no perversion of justice if each deed leads to the necessary results. Freedom of will in its simple form leads to apostasy regarding divine knowledge and ability (omniscience and omnipotence).

R. Moshe Yosef of Narbonne—Moses Narboni (near the end of the thirteenth century)—determines in his article on free will that "as man is able [to act], and God knows everything, this is a contradiction" ("Essay on Freedom of Choice" in *Words of the Wise Sages*, ed. by Eliezer Ashkenazi, cited in Guttmann's *Philosophy of Judaism*). However, he upholds the concept of freedom of choice when he determines that God knows only Himself. *This knowledge indeed includes the knowledge of "everything existing," but not knowledge of partial things.* In accordance with the Aristotelian tradition, R. Narboni negates the existence of total determinism regarding events in our world.

A slightly different approach was taken by *R. Levi ben Gerson* (Ralbag, 1288–1344). Ralbag believed in historical development, but did not ascribe it to continuous divine intervention. He looked for an alternative to the laws determined a priori at creation, and found it in astrology, which he considered empirical science. We can see here a *precedent for the materialistic theory of Karl Marx*, which aimed to anchor progress in the laws inherent in matter. In Ralbag's opinion, all creatures under the sun exist according to the causal predestiny determined by the movement of celestial bodies. However, man has the ability to reflect and decide. This is because he has, to a certain extent, the ability to imagine the future. The influence of celestial bodies does not change, but the result of this influence can change through man's voluntary decisions, and these results can be defined as providence for reward and punishment. If man acts out of correct understanding of the future, he will be rewarded for good, and if he acts out of ignorance, he will be punished. With this mechanical approach, Ralbag relinquishes the religious-moral tenet that was important to Maimonides, i.e., providence expresses reciprocity between man and his God.

R. Hasdai Crescas (1340–1410) supports complete determinism, returning to the Arab philosophical tradition prevalent in the time of Ibn Senna (Avicenna). This theory purports that man's choice is wholly determined by the development of previous causes—inner causes connected to his character, and external causes or factors that influence him. We have already met with this view in the case of Abner of Burgos, but while Abner was alienated from his Judaism for a long time before converting to Christianity, Crescas was completely immersed in Judaism. His advocacy of the theory of predestination thus carries much more weight with respect to Jewish philosophy than Abner's admission on this issue. Crescas admits:

> [A]n event can be said to be possible if looked at merely from the essence of the individual object. In accordance with its essence, the human will can decide one way or another, and in this sense the characterization of the nature of the human will is correct. Similarly, the fact of ethical commandments also presupposes that the nature of human will would not prescribe its mode of action, that human choice is not predetermined. On the other hand determinism is correct if we center our attention, not upon the essence of single individuals, but upon the causes which work upon them. The human will as such has the possibility of many alternatives, but the causes operating on the will determine which course to choose at any given time. If two men were situated in identically similar inner and outer conditions, their decisions would be the same. (Guttmann, 270)

This is definitely not self-evident, as we will explain below.

According to *R. Joseph Albo* (c. 1380–1444), Crescas's position represented a certain deviation from Jewish tradition, and Crescas's pupil, R. Joseph Albo, did not follow in his footsteps. He distinguishes between three types of human actions (*Book of Principles*, article 4):

(1) "Completely voluntary acts—both those in which the nature of the possible is preserved, and those for which man invests diligence and effort, and for which he is praised or condemned. For these acts warning and command will be given, and for them he will receive reward and punishment." Acts of this type are not completely determined by the previous chain of causes. R. Crescas denied the existence of this type.

(2) "Acts that are entirely necessary—both those predetermined due to the system, and those predetermined through Divine Providence...and these things are not controlled at all by human freedom of choice."

(3) Acts "that are a combination of the two types, meaning those determined through predestination and through choice." Acts of this type are the product of the *merging together of man's efforts and Providence*. "*Most of man's acts that are products of Divine Providence over man through reward and punishment follow this form*, i.e., a combination of predestination and choice" (emphasis mine).

According to R. Albo (ibid., 1:9), the assumption of freedom of choice is the "origin (i.e., the principle motivation) of all acts, mutual agreements, and courteous behaviors through which the state is established, without which we cannot manage."

* * *

Above we have presented a short review of the opinions of prominent Jewish philosophers. Most of them were believing, God-fearing Jews who observed the commandments. Yet the spectrum of their opinions is very wide and includes both complete freedom of choice and complete determinism that negates free choice. On this issue, Judaism seems to allow for a spectrum of opinions (within the limits of the main principles).

Understanding this variety of views may pave the way for new approaches to the old paradox. We will devote the next chapter to our own search for a way to comprehend the seeming paradox.

10. A Different Approach to the Paradox of "Everything is foreseen yet freedom of choice is given"

A. Freedom of Choice—A Metaphysical Concept

The concept of freedom of choice can be understood in the context of the law of causality. In general, we explain the law of causality in the following manner. In nature, everything is in a permanent state of movement and transformation. Each event (which may be called the effect) has events that precede it (or a certain event that precedes it) which constitute a cause for this event. For example, banging a table causes noise, and therefore we say that the banging is the cause and the noise is the effect. When we throw a stone up, it falls down. The throwing of the stone is the cause for the fall, and the fall of the stone is the effect. In discussing cause and effect in an absolute manner, a law must connect the two events to each other. In this case, the law of gravity connects the throwing of the stone (cause) and its fall (effect).

Examining the connection between events brings us to the law of causality. It seems as though each event in the world has a cause—prior events caused the later event, which is a result of the previous events. However, there is no proof of the law of causality. Moreover, Hume proved that we cannot logically infer a law of causality through experiment and observations, however many experiments we perform. Hume did not prove the invalidity of the law of causality. He only showed that causality does not stem logically from experiment, according to rational considerations. Thus we may conclude that the law of causality (if such a law exists at all) is a metaphysical law. That is to say, it cannot be refuted either logically or by experiment (whereas a scientific theory can be tested, and although not positively verified, it can potentially be refuted by experiment).

The claim that each event in the world has a cause or a system of causes that unequivocally leads to a certain event is a determinist claim. If a certain event is determined (unequivocally) by previous events, this means that the previous events were also (unequivocally) determined by events prior to them. If we go back to the creation of the world, we conclude that all the events in the world were determined in advance. This conclusion assumes that even intelligent beings, humans, are subject to the law of causality. However, this assumption contradicts the idea of man's free will. If we assume that man has free will, then the world ceases to be determinist, even if matter is subject to total causality. Indeed, how can we determine whether man has freedom of choice? R. Crescas reasons that if two people have equivalent inner and external conditions, they arrive at the same decisions. But this is not convincing and does not constitute a logical proof, for no two persons have identical characterizations of freedom of choice. Moreover, no experiment can verify or negate this difference. If the "inner conditions are equal," we must be speaking about two identical people, and then the claim that they will make identical decisions is not a logical conclusion, but a denial of free will.

Knowledge of free choice is not based on a logical assumption but on immediate knowledge, man's direct experience. I have already quoted Immanuel Kant's view on this subject (in section 1.2): "To argue freedom [of will] away is as impossible for the most abstruse philosophy as it is for the most ordinary human reason." As we cannot prove or disprove the existence of freedom of choice, it is actually a matter of faith. This is a fundamental belief and is deeply rooted in man's awareness, the prototype of faith in God, which is also an immediate and direct experience that cannot be proved logically.

B. Two Types of Development—Material and Spiritual

We have identified two kinds of development: the development of the material world, run by the laws of nature, and the development of the human mind. Regularity in the material world may be subject to the principle of causality. Causality may have a determinist character, such that each event is caused unequivocally by the events that preceded it. However, determinism in the material world is not indispensable—that is to say, the world can be understood without the concept of determinism. An example of regularity that is not determinist is provided by quantum mechanics in which a certain event or system of events may cause possible results. This means there is no law that determines in advance which definite result will be caused from previous events. The laws of quantum mechanics only determine the probabilities of various possibilities.

Development in the sphere of human intelligence has a completely different character. Man's will is what determines which event from a possible range will actually come about. A high school graduate may choose among many possibilities as to a field of further academic or professional study and the location of the academic institution. He chooses one of the possibilities. This is completely different from the indeterminism of quantum mechanics, in which the range of possibilities has a random character, described by the distribution of probability. In contrast, man's decision is generally intelligent; at least it can be intelligent, and what leads to one decision or another is a system of rational considerations. In our example, the possible considerations are a personal interest in a certain profession, the prestige of the institution, the chance of making a living in the chosen profession, and so on. Generally, man's decisions stem also from a system of values, i.e., from his beliefs and his education. It may also be that certain emotions lead to the decision. But also in this case it has nothing to do with the chance-like character of quantum laws.

We identify, therefore, two separate systems: the material world with its laws, the laws of nature; and the human mind and soul. As we indicated earlier, Popper calls the world of the material "world one," and the spiritual "world two." The two worlds are definitely related, and this is dealt with under the rubric of "the psychophysical problem," the problem of body and soul. According to Jewish thought, the world of the soul is connected to God.

In general, our world (which includes both the material world, the spiritual world, and divine providence) is not determinist, and its indeterminism includes man's free will and God's will. This conclusion is independent of the determinism or indeterminism of the material world. The interaction between world two (human mind, soul) and divine providence results in an indeterministic universe.

C. Knowledge of the Future

Can a particular individual know the future? Let us assume that man has freedom of choice. We claim that if an individual knows the future, this contradicts his freedom of choice. A certain chain of events stems from a certain act of free will. Now suppose that in opposition to our previous claim, a certain person can predict the result of the chain of events stemming from a deed he has chosen to do. If he concludes that the result is undesirable, he will probably activate his free will in order to choose another act that will give a different, more desirable result. Since his knowledge of the future is now directly contributing to its alteration (by means of the activation of his free will to change the result), we see that the possibility of a free will choice contradicts the possibility of knowledge of the future. If so, then there is no unambiguous prediction of the future (or, there is no unambiguous future).

For example, a person buys a certain stock and uses his ability to know the future to predict its price next week. If the price of the stock goes down, that person will lose money. The person can change the results of this free choice, which would result in a future monetary loss, by buying a different stock, or not buying any stock at all. In this case, his prediction is faulty. His knowledge of the future leads directly to the exercise of his free will to change it, causing the prediction to be invalid; we arrive at the conclusion that man cannot predict his personal future. Such a prediction contradicts man's free will. However, we may conclude that an individual cannot predict anything at all, for the simple reason that the results of his decisions are dependent on the decisions of other individuals, who are interacting with him in the context of buying the stock. In other words, an individual is not a closed system.

Now we will discuss knowledge of the future within a system, such as a certain human society. This human society is, in certain approximations, a closed system. In any event, we may consider mankind as a closed system (from a certain point of view, since it is open vis-à-vis God). When we talk about a system, we assume mutual influence between its components. In our example, individuals and society have reciprocal influence, exchanging information between them. In society as well, prior knowledge of the future contradicts society's free will to carry out various deeds. Knowledge of the future causes changes of deeds, and this change gives rise to another future. *This means that knowledge of the future changes the future.* Therefore, knowledge of the future is impossible in a system, in society, just as it is impossible for an individual.

Let us take for example America in 1939, and assume that Albert Einstein predicted the realization of the nuclear bomb in 1945. Furthermore, he knew (as part of his knowledge of the future) the details of the manufacture of the bomb. In this situation, Einstein would transmit all the information to other scientists. America would assemble its resources and the nuclear bomb would be ready for action not in 1945, but well before, say in 1940. Assuming that dropping the atom bomb would have caused the defeat of Nazi Germany, the war would have ended in 1940. Again, we arrive at an inner contradiction—knowledge of the future changes the anticipated future.

Note that in this section we have not made use of any theological or religious arguments, but only logical arguments. Our basic premise is that a system is capable of making changes and decisions, and implementing them when new information appears. In the case of an individual, this ability is part of his freedom of choice, and "the system's freedom of choice" is derived from individual freedom of choice.

After demonstrating the impossibility of predicting the future, we ask, how can science make predictions? This raises the issue of the precision of the prediction. Classical physics (not quantum) proposes, in principle, total separation between subject and object. The experimenter (the subject) does not influence the object of the experiment to any serious degree, and we can ignore this influence, which is negligible. An external observer, uninvolved in the system, can, in principle, predict the future. (This is the case assuming that any foreknowledge does not affect the system since the observer does not provide his prediction to the system).

However, classical physics is only an approximation of reality. In truth, the experimenter does make changes to the object of the study. Quantum physics takes into account the mutual influence between subject and object. In the micro-world of elementary particles, there is no total separation between subject, experimental tool, and object. This does not mean that quantum physics cannot predict the future, but the preciseness of the prediction is limited. The well-known uncertainty principle is connected with this limitation.

We began with simple, logical considerations, and end with quantum physics...

We might ask the following: how can we reconcile the above with God's knowledge of the future, which is one of the signs of God's omnipotence? We have shown that precise knowledge of the future within a system, when subject and object are one and the same, contradicts logic. Popper confirms this in *Open Universe*: "Self-prediction is impossible." Similarly, Maimonides asserts that for God there is no distinction between subject and object (see 9B). Here we should clarify that God's omnipotence does not apply to illogical concepts. Maimonides gives the example of a triangle whose angles do not add up to 180 degrees. Such a triangle is a logical contradiction (in Euclidian space) and cannot exist. Accordingly, it would be a mistake to think that because "He cannot" create such a triangle, God's omnipotence has a limit.

The expression "definite divine knowledge of the future" includes an inner logical contradiction, because it implies a limitation on God's omnipotence: definite knowledge of the future would imply He could not change things He Himself had predicted in advance. In addition, intervention in the past is not one of the qualities of God's omnipotence: such a possibility clearly leads to logical contradictions. For example, suppose you were able to take a journey to the past, meet there your mother, and kill her before your birth, or prevent her from marrying your father. This would affect the present, in which you now could not exist. The contradiction is that you are alive, while the intervention in the past leads to your inexistence.

Reducing God's sovereignty over man, such as Rabad suggests, is no solution: if God were not omnipotent then He would not be divine. The impossibility of intervening in the past or of having definite knowledge of the future is not a limitation of God's omnipotence or reduction of His power. Simply, we cannot endow God with illogical qualities (like in the above example of creating a triangle the sum of whose angles does not equal 180 degrees). The concept of "definite divine knowledge of the future" is logically flawed and cannot be applied to descriptions of God.

D. The Future Is Not Explicitly Concealed in the Past

Above we discussed knowledge of the future. This means that at a certain time, in the present, it is possible to define something as the future, and it is possible to know it. In other words, the present, together with the past, is what determines the future. The question we now ask is, is it possible to know the future at all? We cannot know whether the past determines the future (determinism), basing ourselves on experiments or scientific hypotheses. The question of determinism is a metaphysical question. In general, science is not derived from experiment, and metaphysics is not derived from science. As we wrote in chapter 2, science has the status of divine revelation. What is the source of metaphysics? We draw our metaphysical ideas from the same source, divine revelation, which is documented in the Torah.

I anticipate that this definition of metaphysics as based on Torah will attract the fierce opposition of those who call themselves atheists or agnostics. If so, I challenge them to find another source for their metaphysics. Very probably, at least some of their metaphysical assumptions, which seem "self-evident," are actually the product of Jewish culture, and taken from the same source—the Torah. When Albert Einstein tries to prove the determinism of the material world, a metaphysical assumption, he turns to the image of God, saying, "He does not play dice."

An analysis of the metaphysical foundations of modern science cannot be exhausted in one paragraph. E. A. Burtt has devoted a whole book, *The Metaphysical Foundations of Modern Science*, to the thought of such giants as Copernicus, Galileo, and Newton, who laid the metaphysical foundations of modern physics.

Newton (and others, but most prominently him) based the metaphysical foundations of his scientific thought on his religious outlook, which, with regard to the creation of the world and its order, was a direct legacy of Jewish philosophy.

The Torah begins with the creation of the world. The very concept of the creation of the world involves metaphysical projections. If the world has been created, then this world has meaning. On the other hand, if the entire future of the world was concealed in the first instant of creation, as determinism assumes, then the development of the world is superfluous! This means that determinism leads to the conclusion that creation is meaningless. We interpret this negation to mean that the opposite is true: the world is indeterminist. Man is the one who introduces uncertainty to the world. The world cannot be definite and determinist if man has free will (and God's will governs the world). The future is not concealed in the past; the past does not determine the future explicitly.

The Torah clearly emphasizes the truth of these claims:

> God saw that man's wickedness was great upon the earth, and that every product of the thought of his heart was only bad always. God reconsidered having made man upon the earth, and He had heartfelt sadness. (Genesis 6:5–6)
>
> Now the earth had become corrupt before God, and the earth had become filled with robbery. (Ibid., verse 11)

These verses assert that the reality that God created was not concealed—and irrevocably sealed—in the act of creation, but was the result of man's actions through free choice. Here are additional examples:

> If you will follow My decrees and observe My commandments and perform them, then I will provide your rains in their time, and the land will give its produce and the tree of the field will give its fruit.... But if you will not listen to Me and will not perform all of these commandments...your strength will be spent in vain; your land will not give its produce and the tree of land will not give its fruit. (Leviticus 26: 3, 4, 14, 20)
>
> All those men who have tested Me ten times and have not listened to My voice, surely they will not see the Land that I have sworn to give to their forefathers—all who anger Me will not see it. (Numbers 14:22–23)

The Torah unequivocally determines here and elsewhere that future reality is conditioned on man's deeds, and these deeds are the result of man's free choice.

E. Everything Is Foreseen

The Torah attributes meaning and purpose to creation and its development, and grants special meaning to the history of mankind. However, the free will given to every individual may cause significant deviations from the destination determined by God, in which case

God may intervene openly and bring about the necessary correction. Such an intervention is considered a miracle, and the Torah documents a number of such adjustments. One example is the Flood: "I am about to bring the floodwaters upon the land to destroy all flesh" (Genesis 6:17). Another is the Tower of Babel: "And God dispersed them from there over the face of the whole earth, and they stopped building the city" (ibid. 11:8). A third is the Ten Plagues: "See all the wonders that I have put in your hand and perform them before Pharaoh" (Exodus 4:21).

However, we can say that such open interventions are not the rule, but the exception. They characterize the stages of the childhood and youth of mankind and the Jewish people, when men themselves were not yet fully mature. In later stages of historical development (the stage of "maturity") God's open intervention no longer exists. R. Kook understands the word "history" in Hebrew as "hiding": history takes place with God hiding His face. This means that in our modern times, divine providence does not usually intervene openly, and thus it is generally not apparent to us, although it may be felt on a personal level.

We have shown that human history has meaning. Divine providence determines the direction and destination of mankind's development. In Judaism, God is the God of history. God's commandments have historical meaning. Man is the partner of his Creator in the process of human development. However, we still cannot explain how God directs humanity in a certain direction when man has total freedom of choice. The paradox of R. Akiva does not contrast human freedom of choice with divine knowledge of the future of each individual in detail. Rather, the paradox means that *history develops in a direction determined by God, even though each individual has freedom of choice.*

The biblical story demonstrates how a divine plan is implemented despite realization of the conflicting desires of individuals. For example, see the story of Joseph and his brothers in Genesis. Some commentators see the exile of the Israelites from Canaan to the land of Goshen in Egypt as one of the components of the divine plan. In

Canaan, the Israelite minority faced the danger of assimilation into the idol-worshipping Canaanite culture. In Goshen, however, they were able to develop with minimum contact with the local population. Individuals, each with his own desires and free will, carried out this plan. These desires were not always of morally positive intent. Joseph behaved arrogantly towards his brothers. Joseph's brothers wanted to kill him, and in the end, they sold him to the Ishmaelites. Potiphar's wife also did not have good intentions. The Bible is full of such examples. Nevertheless, men and women brought God's plan to fruition with their own hands.

The paradox is that future development is planned in advance (*everything is foreseen*); nevertheless, human beings realize it through their free will (*yet freedom of choice is given*). The assumption that everything is predicted does not contradict Popper's statement, "self-prediction is impossible." As we explained, this sentence refers to precise prediction. Precise prediction means foreseeing the development of each individual, *but prediction of every detail is impossible*. This is the main difficulty in understanding the assumption that "everything is predicted": most have understood this to mean the knowledge of the development of each individual.

The problem is not God's lack of ability to know the future of each individual. An individual who has freedom of choice does not have a definite future, for he can always make choices to change it, whereas for one who has a definite future, morality and commandments have no significance. Thus the knowledge of a definite individual future is a contradiction in terms, for it does not exist. The problem is not our failure to understand the nature of God's knowledge, in Maimonides' words, but that we cannot know an individual's future, as the future does not explicitly exist in the present. We cannot know something that does not exist. The uncertainty of the future is a result of the freedom of choice of each individual. Moreover, general uncertainty of the future for a single person becomes *maximum* uncertainty—that is, a *definite* future for an individual does not and cannot exist in the present.

Man cannot understand and explain everything. Sooner or later, we confront the mystery of the world, which only God knows: "You know all the secrets of the world and the mysteries of each living creature" (liturgy from the Day of Atonement). In order to sharpen the paradox, we will present an allegory based on quantum physics. But this example is more than just an allegory; to those who believe in the unity of the world, an example from the material part of the world may reflect general rules governing both material and spiritual domains. Possibly, the distinction between the two is a result of man's restricted intellectual perception. Apart from this, we are intentionally taking an example from quantum physics, because in quantum physics there isn't a total separation between subject and object.

Below is a description of the two-slit experiment. We need not be experts in quantum mechanics in order to describe this experiment and to understand its implications. We need only know that it can be carried out, and that it has been carried out many times, in different versions. A beam of electrons (or other particles) is sent to a screen

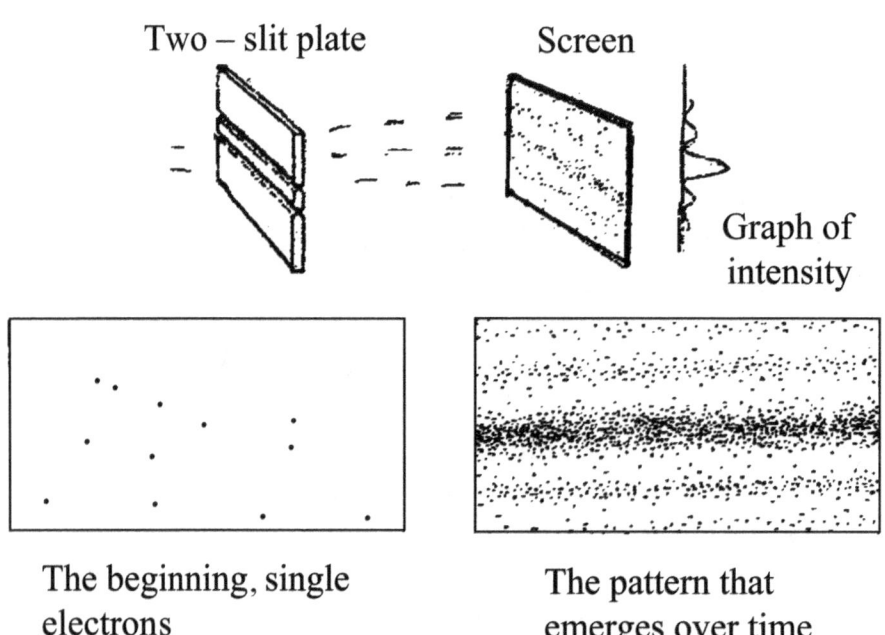

with two slits. Some of the electrons pass through the slit and hit another screen (see the diagram.) We may send the electrons one by one, or many at once. When an electron arrives at the screen, a black dot appears on it. The quantum theory claims that in principle, we cannot predict a certain electron's exact place of contact on the screen. There is no law that governs the path of a certain electron. The theory can only calculate the probability that the electron will arrive at a certain place on the screen, but in order to measure these probabilities, we must send a large number of electrons. Since no law determines the arrival point of a single electron, physicists say (by way of metaphor) that the electron has "freedom of choice."

The electron in this allegory symbolizes man, who has the freedom to choose his path—"freedom of choice is given." What represents "everything is predicted"? If we send a very large number of particles to the screen one after the other through the two-slit board, a wave pattern gradually appears (that does not constitute overlapping, superimposition of the distributions of the particles from each one of the slits, as we might expect; such a superposition would not provide a wave pattern). The laws of quantum physics predict this pattern, even though they cannot predict the path of a single particle.

This example, which describes the real world, is a material illustration of the contradiction between the uncertainty characterizing the individual (the electron) and the certainty characterizing the results of the actions of many individuals.

How does quantum physics (or general physics) explain this strange experiment, which is the focal point of quantum physics? Physics cannot explain it! Richard Feynman writes: "One might still like to ask: 'How does it work? What is the machinery behind the law?' No one has found any machinery behind the law. No one can 'explain' any more than we have just explained [the existence of such experiments and the use of the equations of quantum mechanics]" (*The Feynman Lectures on Physics*, vol. 3, 1–10). Thus, we see that even in physics the paradox exists of "Everything is foreseen, yet freedom of choice is given."

My own understanding of the sentence "everything is predicted" relates not to the future of each individual, but to a divine plan that is carried out and unavoidable, even though the individual has freedom of choice. Here I apply the term "individual" to an entire community as well as to single persons. For example, the second paragraph of the Shema prayer (Deuteronomy 11) states that the fall of the rain ("and I will give rain in your land at its time") depends on whether the Israelites serve God properly.

F. "I Will Be What I Will Be" (Exodus 3:14)

In God's revelation to Moses within the burning bush, Moses asks God to reveal His name. God answers, "I will be what I will be." This phrase has stumped many translators.

One translation (Holy Scriptures, Koren Publishers, 1988) renders it as "I will be ever what I now am." We might conclude from this that "I will be" is irrevocably determined by "what I am now." In other words, the present indisputably determines the future—total determinism. My opinion about the meaning of this phrase is completely different: I propose that it means "I will be what I will be." The future ("I will be") is determined in a future development ("what I will be"). This development is the realization of the divine plan, God's design, by human beings with freedom of choice. Thus God navigates and directs human history. He has determined the general plan in advance (the final picture on the screen in our allegory of the electrons above), but the implementation depends on mankind. During the development of history, new entities and phenomena are created that were not intrinsic in the creations of the past. Historical events that were not determined in advance give rise to new developments. "I will be what I will be" means that the future determines the future, while the divine plan is predetermined.

G. Summary

"Everything is foreseen, yet freedom of choice is given" is understood by many Jewish philosophers as a contradiction between God's omnipotent knowledge of the individual's future, and man free will. I do not purport to solve this paradox. However, in my opinion, this paradox is located in a contradiction of a different sort.

Maimonides already noted that knowledge of the future is impossible because we cannot separate subject from object. Maimonides concluded that man cannot understand the character of divine knowledge. In this way, Maimonides absolves himself of solving the paradox. He sees no contradiction between freedom of choice, something that we can claim to understand, and knowledge of God, which we are incapable of understanding. In contrast, Rabad assumes that God limits his ability to know the future. Other Jewish philosophers advocate various approaches and types of metaphysics, among them the extreme views of Abner and R. Crescas—full determinism and negation of man's freedom of choice. My approach relies on the assumption that we cannot attribute illogical qualities to God. Precise self-prediction in a context of freedom of choice contradicts logic. Because vis-à-vis God there is no clear separation between subject and object, the assumption of precise knowledge of the future by God is illogical.

The Creator gave man the vital quality of freedom of choice. Because our world contains beings with free choice, it is indeterminist. The future is not unequivocally determined according to the past. *We cannot predict the future, as the future itself is not explicitly determined.* This is true in general, but for the individual it has particular meaning—an individual's freedom of choice causes uncertainty regarding that individual's future. We cannot know anything that does not yet exist. Since the individual's future definitely does not yet exist, and is certainly not determined in the present (since freedom of choice exists), then the future cannot be determined with certainty. Man brings uncertainty into the world, and men are the ones who determine historical development. Each person has his own will, and men's wills can be conflicting. They have the freedom of choice to implement their intentions and desires at least partially and within the system of life's constraints.

The true paradox in the expression "everything is foreseen, yet freedom of choice is given" is not divine knowledge of the future in contrast to human free choice, but implementation of the divine plan vis-à-vis individual freedom of choice. The true meaning of the assertion "everything is foreseen" is, in my opinion, the existence of a divine plan, a destination for historical development. Both the Torah and the laws of nature determine the limits of "everything is predicted." *The real paradox is how the divine plan is carried out within human history through human deeds, given that men have conflicting desires and complete freedom of choice.* The example we gave from quantum mechanics illustrates the realization of this paradox in the inanimate world.

Chapter Five

Conclusion

1. *Blind Faith versus Rationality*

We have examined two conflicting world perspectives, and concluded that one relies on blind faith, while the second is rational. We described the confrontation between these two worldviews. Which of them is the perspective of blind faith, and which is rational? We identified blind faith in the materialistic, naturalist perception, and in the secular perception in general, which is devoid of God. In contradistinction, the rational perspective is the viewpoint of the Torah and Jewish thought.

A. Mind and Body

We started with the most important thing for every person: his soul. The concepts of soul and free will are interrelated, and foreign to the material world. According to the materialist, naturalist viewpoint, everything in the world, including my inner world or self, is inferred from matter and the physical world, including light, photons, and all other elementary particles.

This *blind faith* does not rely on any experimental or theoretical proof. It is as if someday in the future scientists will prove that our brain *determines* our thoughts and that one's mind is identical with his brain. Our daily language testifies that we have already become accustomed to this idea, as we talk about *an analytical brain, a Jewish brain,* and so on.

Indeed this is blind faith. Why did we call this approach irrational? We devoted the first part of the book to this topic. Here I will review certain aspects of the problem. This is a metaphysical topic. The materialist viewpoint of the issue is metaphysical, as is the viewpoint of Jewish philosophy. This means that we cannot infer them from experiment, just as we cannot infer metaphysics from science or scientific theories. In any case, we can assess whether or not a certain metaphysical approach is rational. How so?

Let us assume, following the materialist dogma, that matter (the brain) determines our thoughts. This assumption—that neither logical reason nor faith determines our behavior, but the movement of atoms and molecules within the brain—has irrational ramifications. I repeat Popper's statement:

> I do not claim that I have refuted materialism. But I do think I have shown that materialism has no right to claim that it can be supported by rational argument—argument that is rational by logical principles. Materialism can be true, but it is incompatible with rationalism, with the acceptance of the standards of critical argument: for the standards appear from the materialist point of view as an illusion or, at least, as ideology. (*The Self and Its Brain*, 81)

The materialistic viewpoint is nothing more than blind faith; it is irrational. We showed above that all secular faith is irrational, and we will return to this later.

We emphasized that there is nothing more real in the world than *my own self.* As Russell said, "I hold that whatever we know without inference is mental." The Jews accepted belief in one God as God's revelation, and they bequeathed this faith to all of mankind. This belief connects my soul with divine intelligence, with the infinite mind, and not with matter as materialism teaches us. Judaism is not blind faith; it is based on the numerous biblical testimonies documenting connection with the divine. This faith does not lack rationality, as does materialism. The irrationality of materialism stems from the belief that human intelligence is connected to matter, and matter directs intelligence. The Jewish alternative connects human intelligence to the infinite mind of God. This connection is a guarantee of the rationality of the Jewish approach.

B. Science

Popper sees himself as a *secular* realist. He and other secular philosophers criticized materialism with great success, and exposed its irrationality. What is the meaning of secularism? In the introductory chapter, we gave a dictionary definition: "Not holy, unconnected to religion, to the holiness of faith." A non-materialistic secular approach that recognizes the reality of two entities, matter and spirit, does not meet the criteria of scientific cognition. Einstein and Popper admit that the fact that we have some understanding of the world is the greatest of miracles in the universe. Herein lies the bankruptcy of the secular approach, the admission of its irrationality. If the discovery of a basic theory is a miracle, as Popper says, then a secular explanation for scientific cognition is not rational. Just as materialism did not pass the test posed by the problem of body and soul, so the secular, general (that is, non-materialistic) approach did not pass the test of the problem of understanding the world.

Judaism suggests a rational explanation for the problem of understanding the world (see chapter 2 above and my article "Comprehensibility of the World: the Jewish Outlook," *BDD* [Bar Ilan University] 9 [Summer 1999]: 5–21). Human intelligence alone is not capable of discovering a new theory *ex nihilo*. Indeed, according to Jewish perception, an infinite mind is attached to the human mind. A discovery of a new theory is, in fact, a divine revelation. The greatest of the secular philosophers, including Hume, Kant, and

Popper, saw this as an unsolvable puzzle—how can a new scientific theory arise? However, Judaism gives a rational explanation for this.

When we ignore the divine source of our knowledge (or do not notice it), we are afflicted by blind faith in the laws of nature. We assume that we have succeeded, through intuition or miraculous chance, in proposing a theory that corresponds exactly to all the experiments. Where do we get the confidence that this theory will allow correct prediction of future experiments, or even for only one of them? There is no rational proof for the prediction of the future based on any theory, and the principle of induction is incorrect. According to the secular perspective, it is no more than blind faith. In general, the secular approach to scientific cognition is irrational, and consists of blind faith. In contrast, Judaism provides a rational explanation.

C. Evolution

The fact that a chain of events took place in the development of life on earth does not prove the truth of the theory of evolution. Even if the chain of events has an evolutionary character, this is not sufficient to establish a law of nature. A one-time historical event is not enough to establish a law of nature, nor does a past process of evolution prove evolution in the future. As Popper says:

> There exists no law of evolution, only the historical fact that plants and animals change, or more precisely, that they have changed. The idea of a law which determines the direction and the character of evolution is a typical nineteenth-century mistake, arising out of the general tendency to ascribe to the 'Natural Law' the functions traditionally ascribed to God. (*Conjectures and Refutations*, 340)

Indeed, there is no law of evolution. So what is there? Here I have to explain an important general point. The term "evolution" applies to every slow and gradual change of an entity. There are two paradigms of development. One follows the laws of nature, such as cosmological theories. The second paradigm relates to the lives of man, the biography and history of humans. Characterizing this second paradigm is the concept of *creatio ex nihilo* [creation out of nothing] or openness to God. Evolution includes many instances that fall under the rubric of creation: of life itself, of various species, of man with his creativity and freedom of choice, of creations of human genius. These—and numerous other examples—are creations *ex nihilo*.

A rational account that explains *creatio ex nihilo* and points to development in general can be subsumed under one of the fundamental concepts of Judaism—divine providence. Not the law of evolution, but rather divine providence is what runs the development of life on earth.

In contrast, the secular approach is not capable of providing a metaphysical, rational basis for a *creatio ex nihilo* reality, but defines it as a miracle.

D. History

Clearly, we cannot describe historical development according to a paradigm of the first type. There is no law-like regularity, trajectory, or trend in history. These concepts are the inventions of the materialistic schools, and they are obsolete. However, the "secular intelligentsia" refuses to recognize this.

The alternative is to understand the role of divine providence in history. However, this alternative contains the paradox of "everything is foreseen, yet freedom of choice is given." The God who created man granted him the free will to choose. God causes mankind to march towards a predetermined destination—everything is predicted. But He has placed the realization of this destination in the hands of freely-choosing man; thus freedom of choice is given. The secret of divine providence is in the unseen confrontation between God and man, as well as the participation of man in the divine drama.

Freedom of choice means that man himself determines the stages of his future. Each stage in the future depends on man's choice, but the results of man's acts also depend on existing limitations. An individual's future is not implicit in the present and in the past, and since we cannot in the present know something that does not (yet) exist, we cannot know the individual's future.

God's knowledge, "*everything is foreseen,*" indicates a destination, a divine plan. For centuries, Jewish philosophers attributed knowledge of an individual's future to God, and saw in this knowledge a paradox, standing in contradiction to the assumption that "*freedom of choice is given.*" But in my opinion, the true paradox, which contains the essence of divine providence, lies in the question of how God's *design* is realized within human history through man, with his various desires and his freedom of will.

2. *The Self and the Quest for Meaning*

> If I am not for myself, who will be for me? And when I am for myself, what am I? And if not now, when? (Ethics of the Fathers 1:14)

In my searching, I have read numerous books on Jewish and general philosophy. The conundrum of men's free will has continued to fascinate me. Free will is not a phenomenon from within the field of science and does not agree with the materialistic approach.

Within myself, within my *self*, I felt the struggle between two poles: my faith on the one hand, and materialist, rationalist science on the other. I identified the need for an impartial analysis of the structure and status of science and materialism. For me, such an analysis would be the spiritual improvement that Hillel referred to when he said, "If I am not for myself, who will be for me?"

This conflict has another dimension. In many circles, science is considered a substitute for religion, and this implies that science threatens religion. I have been a scientist all my life. I was educated in the Soviet Union and I studied the theory of materialism in depth.

Yet from this background sprang a new purpose involving research and creativity in a field quite different from that of my life-long research. I published an article, "Comprehensibility of the World: Jewish Outlook," in which I demonstrated the divine source of scientific inspiration.

The publication of this article was the first stage in the overall program I had outlined for myself: to analyze the conflict between two worldviews, secularism and Judaism. The article describes and discusses the secular materialistic worldview, which science supposedly confirms. Here I will engage in a metaphysical speculation. I cannot ignore the impression that my entire previous life served to prepare me for this new mission I have adopted. In my scientific work, I researched a number of topics that did not produce organized results in the form of scientific articles. Among these subjects are the theory of general relativity and biophysics. My study of these topics, together with my knowledge of theoretical physics, my main field of research and publication, provided me with a broad basis for work in my new field of interest.

In this book, I present my preliminary findings. I plan to continue my studies in this area, God willing.

To conclude my thoughts, I will attempt to define the essence of the new understanding I have achieved.

Beyond the material world lies another reality, which is no less real and objective. This is the divine reality, the spiritual reality. Cleaving to God and contact with the reality of the divine is what enables human beings to fulfill the definition of man created "in the image of God."

Regarding the verse, "But you who cling to Hashem, your God—you are all alive today" (Deut. 4:4), R. Kook writes (*Shabbat Ha-Aretz*): "The uniqueness of the people of Israel is that they look at all of existence from the illuminating aspect of the divine. As long as they live, they recognize that life is worthwhile only to the extent that it is divine.... They also know that truly, there is no life but divine life, and life that is not divine is no life at all."

"Cleaving to God" does not mean some kind of mystical unity disconnected from reality. Above all, cleaving to God involves new creation, *ex nihilo*. Innovation is the key to the meaning of life. Clearly, we do not create new things every day. Someone asked Einstein what method he used in order to organize his ideas. He answered that he did not need any method, because new ideas came so rarely. The very aspiration to create the new in building one's own life (as well as in dealing with the outside world) by itself grants meaning to life. Especially when man understands that in this he realizes intimacy with God.

As long as we create, we fulfill our role in life. Consciously or unconsciously, in creating something new, a person realizes his relationship with God. This is true not only in the realms of Torah, science, and art, but first and foremost in our own lives, our most important creations.

Bibliography

Atlas, Samuel. *From Critical to Speculative Idealism: The Philosophy of Solomon Maimon.* The Hague: Martinus Nijhoff, 1964.

Aviezer, Nathan. *In the Beginning... Biblical Creation and Science.* Hoboken, NJ: KTAV Publishing House, 1990.

Bergman, Samuel Hugo. *The Philosophy of Solomon Maimon.* Translated from the Hebrew by Noah J. Jacobs. Jerusalem: The Magnes Press, 1967.

Berkovits, Eliezer. *Faith after the Holocaust.* New York: KTAV Publishing House, 1973.

—. *God, Man and History.* Jerusalem: Shalem Press, 2004.

Burtt, Edwin A. *The Metaphysical Foundations of Modern Science.* Atlantic Highlands, NJ: Humanities Press, 1996.

Darwin, Charles. *The Origin of Species.* London: John Murray, 1859; New York: Bantam Classics, 1999.

Descartes, Rene. *Descartes: Key Philosophical Writings.* Translated by Elisabeth Haldane. Edited by Enrique Chavez-Arvizo. Hertfordshire: Wordsworth Classics, 1997.

Carmell, Aryeh, and Cyril Domb, eds. *Challenge: Torah Views on Science and Its Problems.* Jerusalem: Feldheim, 1978.

Eccles, J. C. *Facing Reality: Philosophical Adventures by a Brain Scientist.* New York: Springer-Verlag, 1970.

Einstein, A. *Ideas and Opinions.* New York: Crown, 1979.
—. *The Meaning of Relativity.* London: Methuen, 1956.
Fackenheim, Emil L. *God's Presence in History.* New York: New York University Press, 1970.
—. *The Jewish Return into History: Reflections in the Age of Auschwitz and a New Jerusalem.* New York: Schocken Books, 1978.
—. *Quest for Past and Future.* Boston: Beacon Press, 1968.
—. *What Is Judaism?* New York: Summit Books, 1987.
Fain, Benjamin. "Comprehensibility of the World: Jewish Outlook." *BDD [Bekhol Derakhekha Deahu] Journal of Torah and Scholarship* 9 (1999): 5–21.
—. *Irreversibilities in Quantum Mechanics.* Dordrecht, Netherlands: Kluwer Academic Publishers, 2000. (See specifically chapter 6, "Quantum Measurement and Irreversibility.")
—, and Mervin F. Verbit. *Jewishness in the Soviet Union: Report of an Empirical Survey.* Jerusalem: Jerusalem Center for Public Affairs/Tarbut, 1984.
Feynman, Richard, Robert B. Leighton, and Matthew Sands. *The Feynman Lectures on Physics.* Vol. 3. London: Addison-Wesley, 1965.
Fox, M., ed. *Modern Jewish Ethics: Theory and Practice.* Columbus: Ohio State University Press, 1975.
Fukuyama, Francis. *The End of History and the Last Man.* London: Penguin Books, 1992.
Gödel, Kurt. *On Formally Undecidable Propositions of Principia Mathematica and Related Systems.* Translated by B. Meltzer. New York: Basic Books, 1962.
Gould, Stephen J. *Wonderful Life: The Burgess Shale and the Nature of History.* London: Penguin Books, 1989.
Guttmann, Julius. *Philosophies of Judaism.* Translated by David Silverman. New York: Schocken Books, 1973.
Hadamard, Jacques. *The Psychology of Invention in the Mathematical Field.* New York: Dover Books, 1954.

Haldane, J. B. S. *The Inequality of Man.* Harmondsworth, Eng.: Penguin Books, 1937.

Hardy, Alister. *The Living Stream.* London: Collins, 1965.

Hume, David A. *A Treatise of Human Nature.* Edited by L. A. Selby-Bigge. Oxford: Clarendon Press, 1888. (Russian translation, 1996.)

Ish-Shalom, Benjamin. *Rav Avraham Itzhak HaCohen Kook: Between Rationalism and Mysticism.* Albany: State University of New York Press, 1993.

Kant, Immanuel. *Critique of Practical Reason.* Chicago: University of Chicago Press, 1949.

—. *Critique of Pure Reason.* London: Macmillan, 1923.

—. *Groundwork of the Metaphysic of Morals.* Translated by H. J. Paton. New York: Harper Torchbooks, 1964.

—. *Prolegomena to Any Future Metaphysics.* New York: Liberal Arts Press, 1950.

Koestler, Arthur. *The Ghost in the Machine.* London: Hutchinson, 1967.

Lamm, N. *Torah Umadda: The Encounter of Religious Learning and Worldly Knowledge in the Jewish Tradition.* Northvale, NJ: Jason Aronson, 1990.

Lewis, Sinclair. *It Can't Happen Here.* New York: Doubleday, 1935.

Maimon, Solomon. *An Autobiography.* Edited and with a preface by Moses Hadas. New York: Schocken Books, 1965.

Maimonides, Moses. *The Guide of the Perplexed.* 2 vols. Translated by Shlomo Pines. Chicago: University of Chicago Press, 1963.

Mayr, Ernst. *One Long Argument: Charles Darwin and the Genesis of Modern Evolutionary Thought.* Cambridge, MA: Harvard University Press, 1993.

Monod, Jacques. *Chance and Necessity: An Essay on the Natural Philosophy of Modern Biology.* London: Penguin Books, 1997.

Nagel, Ernest, and James R. Newman. *Gödel's Proof.* New York: New York University Press, 1958.

Penfield, Wilder. *The Mystery of the Mind.* Princeton: Princeton University Press, 1975.

Penrose, Roger. *The Emperor's New Mind: Concerning Computers, Minds and the Laws of Physics.* London: Vintage, 1990.

Plato. *Apology. The Laws. Meno. Phaedo. The Republic. Timaeus.*

Popper, Karl R. *Conjectures and Refutations: The Growth of Scientific Knowledge.* London: Routledge, 1995.

—. *Knowledge and the Body-Mind Problem: In Defence of Interaction.* London: Routledge, 2000.

—. *The Logic of Scientific Discovery.* London: Routledge, 1992.

—. *Objective Knowledge: An Evolutionary Approach.* Oxford: Clarendon Press, 1995.

—. *The Open Society and Its Enemies.* Vol. 1, *The Spell of Plato.* Vol. 2, *The High Tide of Prophesy: Hegel, Marx, and the Aftermath.* London: Routledge, 1999.

—. *The Open Universe: An Argument for Indeterminism.* London: Routledge, 1995.

—. *The Poverty of Historicism.* London: Routledge, 1999.

—. *Quantum Theory and the Schism in Physics.* London: Routledge, 1995.

—. *Realism and the Aim of Science.* Routledge, 1994.

—. *Unended Quest: An Intellectual Autobiography.* London: Routledge, 1993.

—, and John C. Eccles. *The Self and Its Brain: An Argument for Interaction.* London: Routledge, 1995.

Radkowsky, Dr. Alvin. "The Faith of an Orthodox Jewish Scientist Revisited." *B'Or Ha'Torah* 1 (1982): 22.

Russell, Bertrand. *A History of Western Philosophy, and Its Connection with Political and Social Circumstances from the Earliest Times to the Present Day.* New York: Simon and Schuster, 1945.

—. *Human Knowledge, Its Scope and Limits.* London: George Allen and Unwin, 1948.

Scholem, Gershom. *On Jews and Judaism in Crisis.* New York: Schocken Books, 1976.

Schrödinger, Erwin. *Mind and Matter.* Cambridge: Cambridge University Press, 1959.

—. *What Is Life?* Cambridge: Cambridge University Press, 1948.

Schroeder Gerald L. *Genesis and the Big Bang.* New York: Bantam Books, 1990.

—. *The Science of God.* New York: The Free Press, 1997.

Simpson, George G. *The Meaning of Evolution.* New York: New American Library, 1951.

Soloveitchik, Rabbi Joseph B. *Fate and Destiny: From Holocaust to the State of Israel.* [Translation by L. Kaplan of the Hebrew *Kol Dodi Dofek.*] Hoboken, NJ: KTAV Publishing House, 2000.

—. *Halakhic Man.* Philadelphia: Jewish Publication Society of America, 1983.

—. *The Lonely Man of Faith.* Northvale, NJ: Jason Aronson, 1997.

Spero, Shubert. "Rabbi Joseph Dov Soloveitchik and the Philosophy of Halakha." *Tradition* 30, no. 2 (1996): 45.

Squires, Euan J. *Conscious Mind in the Physical World.* Philadelphia: Institute of Physics Publishing, 1996.

Thorpe, William H. *Biology, Psychology and Belief.* Cambridge: Cambridge University Press, 1961.

—. *Purpose in a World of Chance.* Oxford: Oxford University Press, 1978.

Whitehead, Alfred N. *Adventures of Ideas.* New York: The Free Press, 1967.

—. *Science and the Modern World.* New York: Macmillan, 1935.

In Hebrew:

Agassi, Yosef. *Toldot ha-filosofiah ha-chadashah* [The history of modern philosophy]. Tel Aviv: Tel Aviv University, 1993.

Ben Shlomo, Yosef. *"Shirat ha-chaim": Prakim be-mishnato shel ha-Rav Kook* [Song of life: Selections from the teachings of R. Kook]. Tel Aviv: The Ministry of Defense, 1989.

Ha-Encyclopedia ha-Ivrit [The Hebrew encyclopedia]. Jerusalem: Massada and Encyclopaedia Publishing Co., 1949–1980.

Kook, Rabbi Avraham Yitzhak Hakohen. *Orot ha-kodesh* [Lights of holiness]. 4 vols. Jerusalem: Mossad HaRav Kook, 1992.

Leibowitz, Yeshayahu. *Guf ve-nefesh: Ha-beayah ha-psycho-fisit* [Body and mind: The psychophysical problem]. Tel Aviv: The Ministry of Defense, 1989.

—. *Sichot al mada ve-arakhim* [Discussions on science and values]. Tel Aviv: The Ministry of Defense, 1989.

—, and Yosef Agassi. *Sichot al ha-filosofiah shel ha-mada* [Conversations concerning the philosophy of science]. Edited by Chemi Ben-Noon. Tel Aviv: The Ministry of Defense, 1997.

—, and Yosef Agassi. *Migbalot ha-sechel* [The limits of reason]. Edited by Chemi Ben-Noon. Jerusalem: Keter Publishing House, 1997.

Maimon, Solomon. *Ha-masah al ha-filosofiah ha-transzendentalit* [Essay on transcendental philosophy]. Translated and edited by Shmuel H. Bergman and Nathan Rottenstreich. Jerusalem: Hebrew University, 1941.

—. *Sefer chayey Shlomo Maimon* [The biography of Solomon Maimon]. Translated by Y. L. Baruch. Tel Aviv: Mosad Bialik, 1942.

Rosenberg, Shalom. *Tov ve-ra ba-hagut ha-yehudit* [Good and evil in Jewish philosophy]. Tel Aviv: The Ministry of Defense, 1985.

Sagi, Avi, ed. *Emunah bi-zemanim mishtanim: Al mishnato shel ha-Rav Yosef Dov Soloveitchik* [Faith in changing times: The teachings of R. Joseph Dov Soloveitchik]. Jerusalem: Eliner Library Department of Religious Education and Culture in the Diaspora, 1996.

—. *Yahadut: Bein dat le-musar* [Judaism: Between religion and morality]. Jerusalem: Hakibbutz Hameuchad, 1998.

Scholem, Gershom. *Devarim be-go* [Explications and implications]. Tel Aviv: Am Oved, 1990.

Schweid, Eliezer. *Ha-filosofim ha-gedolim shelanu* [Our great philosophers]. Tel Aviv: Yediot Aharonot: Sifrei Hemed, 1999.

Soloveitchik, Rabbi Joseph B. *Ha-adam ve-olamo* [Man and his world]. Jerusalem: Eliner Library Department of Religious Education and Culture in the Diaspora, 1998.

—. *Ish ha-emunah* [Man of faith]. Jerusalem: Mossad HaRav Kook, 1992.

—. *Ish ha-halakhah: Galui ve-nistar* [Halakhic man: Revealed and hidden]. Jerusalem: Hahistadrut Hatzionit Haolamit, 1992. (See specifically "*U-bikashtem mi-sham*" [From there shall you seek]).

Index

A
Abner of Burgos   151–52, 153, 169
Abraham   125, 129–30
Akiva, Rabbi   10, 146, 147, 164
Albo, Joseph   154
Algorithm   46, 47, 77
Amino acids   91–94, 95, 96
A priori concepts   49, 51, 55, 70, 71, 72, 121
Atheism   11, 40, 55, 59, 61, 87, 115–116
Aviezer, Nathan   8

B
Baal Shem Tov   63
Bell, John S.   107
Ben Shlomo, Y.   148
Berkowitz, Eliezer   137
Biblical criticism   35, 84

Big Bang Theory   32, 83, 108, 114
Bohr, Niels   8, 28, 74
Born, Max   28
Burtt, Edwin A.   162

C
Canaan   164–65
Carley, W.W   103
Causality   48, 151–52, 155–56, 157
Chardin Telhard de, Pierrre   108
Christianity   119, 130, 133, 138
Churchill, Winston   138
Correspondence principle   74, 83
Creation   31, 32–33, 56, 60, 83, 109, 117, 144, 162, 175
Creative Emergent Evolution, 107–11
Creativity   109, 175, 178
Crescas, Hasdai   153, 156, 169

D

Darwin, Charles 39, 85, 86, 96–97, 112, 113, 121
Darwinism 39, 86, 87–88, 112, 116
Deduction 42, 46, 51, 121
Descartes, Rene 27
Determinism 21, 22, 25, 105, 110, 152, 153, 154, 155, 156, 157, 161, 162, 168, 169
Dirac, Paul 28
DNA 39, 91, 93–94, 95–98, 113, 117, 124
Dualism 10, 27, 28, 62, 63

E

Eccles, John C. 21
Egypt 164
Einstein, Albert 7–8, 27, 28, 32, 37, 41, 48, 51, 52, 53, 54, 55, 59, 62, 71, 72, 73, 74, 75–76, 107, 114, 134, 135, 162, 173, 178
Electron 166–67
Eldrige, Niles 100
Engels, Friedrich 86, 108, 112, 119, 120
Enzyme 91, 95
Epistemology 42
Euclidean geometry 46, 47, 48
Evolution 9, 10, 39, 85–86, 87–88, 89, 90, 99, 100–102, 103, 104, 105–7, 112–15, 117, 174–75

F

Fackenheim, Emil L. 72, 136
Feynman, Richard 28–30, 33–39, 167
Fichte, Johann Gottlieb 63
Fox, Marvin
Freedom of will, choice 1, 15–18, 39, 80, 81, 105, 106, 110, 113–14, 115, 116, 117, 125, 137, 145, 146–56, 158, 160, 163, 164, 165, 169–70, 171, 175–176
Freud, Sigmund 85, 121
Fukuyama, Francis 120, 134
Future 44, 45, 50, 74, 111, 120, 147, 153, 158–63, 165, 168, 169, 174, 175–76

G

Gauss, Carl Friedrich 47–48, 77
Gödel, Kurt 46–47
Gödel theorem 45–47
Gould, Stephen J. 100, 102

H

Hadamard, Jacques 77
Halakhah 124, 128
Haldane, John 21, 22, 25
Halevi, Yehuda 150–51
Hanina, Rabbi 17
Hegel, Georg W.F. 119, 120
Heredity 88–89, 90, 112
Heisenberg, Werner 28
Hilbert, David 46

Hillel 176
History 10, 39, 87, 119–70, 163, 164, 168, 175–76
Holocaust 16, 84, 136–37
Humanism 72, 127, 128, 130
Hume, David 8, 42–43, 44, 45, 47, 48, 50, 51, 69, 71–72, 121, 155–56, 173

I
Ibn daud, Abraham [Ben David]. *See Rabad*
Identity, theory 22
Immortality 149
Induction 42–45, 49–53, 81, 174
Intelligence 11, 47, 62, 70, 72, 141, 173
Islam 130, 133, 149

J
Jacob, Francois 101
Joseph 164, 165
Judaism 10, 14nn, 17–18, 31, 40, 56–63, 78–84, 86–87, 88, 105, 111, 112, 114, 119, 120, 124, 128–30, 132–33, 135, 136–40, 141, 146, 158, 162–63, 172–73, 177

K
Kabbalah 28, 34, 87
Kant, Immanuel 17, 18, 45, 47–50, 51, 52, 53, 63, 66–67, 69, 70, 71, 72, 82, 120, 121, 156, 173
Kiev 15–16
Knowledge 26, 31–32, 35, 41, 43, 48–49, 56, 68, 69, 72, 74, 76, 82, 83, 123–25, 126–27, 140–41, 142–44, 147–48, 149–51, 169, 174
Kook, Rav Abraham Itzhak HaCohen 60–61, 164, 177
Kuzari 150

L
Leibowitz, Yeshayahu 21, 26, 41
Levi, ben Gerson (Ralbag) 152–53
Lewis, Sinclair 136
Lichtenstein, Aharon 130
Lwoff, Andre 101

M
Maimon, Solomon 52, 63–69, 72–73
Maimonides 17, 38–39, 56, 58, 59–60, 69, 73, 78–79, 80, 87, 127, 130, 146–48, 151, 153, 160, 165, 169
Marx, Karl 85, 86, 112, 119, 120, 121, 153
Marxism 18, 85, 120
Materia 19, 20, 25, 28, 86, 87
Materialism, dialectical, historical 9–10, 18–20, 21–26, 36, 57, 62, 63, 117, 172, 173, 176

Mayr, Ernst   112
Mendelssohn, Moses   63
Metaphysics   17, 18, 21, 62–63, 72, 73, 79, 83, 101, 104, 105, 111, 122, 135, 161–62, 172
Mind-body problem   13–15, 21–26, 37, 38, 158, 183
Monod, Jacques   101, 108, 118
Monotheism   132
Moses   125
Mutation   89, 90, 104, 112
Mysticism   28, 73, 144

N
Nachmanides   128–29
Narboni, Moses   152
Newton, Isaac   28, 44, 47, 50, 51, 52, 53, 54, 55, 59, 71, 74, 75, 76, 162
Nicolle, Charles   77
Nietzsche, Friedrich   121
Non-determinism   106, 110
Nucleotides   93–94

O
Objectivity   10–11, 26
Object-subject relation   160, 166, 169

P
Parallelism   22
Penrose, Roger   23, 54
Philo of Alexandria   149
Physicalism   19, 21, 26

Planck, Max   28
Plato   27–28
Polynucleotides   93, 94, 97
Polypeptides   91, 93
Popper, Karl   8, 10, 13, 19, 21, 23, 26–30, 39, 41, 43, 44, 45, 50–53, 54–55, 59, 62, 63, 70, 71, 72, 73, 74, 75, 100–101, 102, 109, 111, 118, 121, 122, 123, 127, 140, 141, 143, 144, 158, 160, 172, 173, 174
Predestination   149, 152, 153, 154
Proteins   91–93, 94, 95–96
Providence   10, 11, 35, 86–87, 103–5, 137, 140–41, 142–43, 145, 146–47, 153, 154, 175, 176
Punctuated equilibrium   100

Q
Quantum processes   10–11 (processes), 25, 157, 160, 166
Quantum theory   55, 76, 110, 167

R
Rabad   151, 161, 169
Rabbeinu Bahya   150
Radkowsky, Alvin   144
Rationalism   21 check for earlier, 62–63, 73, 172
Realism   26, 32, 109
Reason   8, 61, 62
Reductionism   19–21, 32, 106
Relativity   27, 48, 51, 55, 59, 73, 76

Ribosome   95
RNA   91, 95–96
Rosenberg, Shalom   136
Russell, Bertrand   36, 42, 45, 49–50, 69, 172

S
Saadia Gaon   149–50
Sagi, Avi   128
Sakharov, Andrei   131–32
Schroeder, Gerald   8
Schrödinger, Erwin   11, 28
Scholem, Gershom   142
Secularism   9, 30–31, 57, 59, 68, 87, 173, 177
Selection, natural   85, 88. 89–90, 100, 102, 103–4, 105, 110, 112, 116–17
Self   10, 11, 15, 23, 26, 28, 36–37, 38, 62, 81, 106, 142, 143, 144, 171, 172, 176
Self-prediction   140, 159
Shneur Zalman of Liadi   83
Simpson, George   102
Solipsism   116
Soloveitchik, Joseph. B., Rabbi   8–9, 34, 38, 39, 41–42, 60, 61, 73, 81–82, 83, 87, 141
Soviet Union   15–18, 131, 138–39, 140, 142, 176
Spencer, Herbert   108
Spero, Shubert   60
Squires, Euan   20
Synthetic, a priori statement   49, 50, 68, 70, 72, 73

T
Truth   21, 26, 51, 53, 76, 81, 82, 83, 132
Two-slit experiment   166–67

W
Whitehead, Alfred   134
Wigner, Eugen   54
Wiesel, Eli   136
Worlds 1, 2 and 3   19, 26–30, 33, 39, 123, 124, 125, 127, 130, 132, 140, 141–43, 144, 158

www.ingramcontent.com/pod-product-compliance
Lightning Source LLC
LaVergne TN
LVHW061331060426
835512LV00013B/2607